A VISUAL HISTORY OF MOTOR HOMES

This book is dedicated to my granddaughter;

Olivia Rose Jenkinson born 1 August 2022

FRONT COVER: 1991 Swift Kon-Tiki

REAR COVERS (LEFT TO RIGHT): 1979 Ci Motorhome MK3/1984 Autohomes UK – Bambi/1978 A – Line Adventura

MAIN IMAGE: 2008 Ace Roma motorhome

A VISUAL HISTORY OF MOTOR HOMES

PHOTOGRAPHS FROM THE 20s to MODERN DAY

ANDREW JENKINSON

WHITE OWL
AN IMPRINT OF PEN & SWORD BOOKS LTD.
YORKSHIRE – PHILADELPHIA

First published in Great Britain in 2025 by
Pen and Sword WHITE OWL
An imprint of
Pen & Sword Books Ltd
Yorkshire - Philadelphia

Copyright © Andrew Jenkinson, 2025

ISBN 978 1 39909 235 7

The right of Andrew Jenkinson to be identified as author of this work has been asserted by him in accordance with the Copyright, Designs and Patents Act 1988.

A CIP catalogue record for this book is available from the British Library.

All rights reserved. No part of this book may be reproduced or transmitted in any form or by any means, electronic or mechanical including photocopying, recording or by any information storage and retrieval system, without permission from the Publisher in writing.

Typeset in 12/14 pts Cormorant Infant
by SJmagic DESIGN SERVICES, India.

Printed and bound by Printworks Global Ltd, London/Hong Kong.

Pen & Sword Books Ltd. incorporates the imprints of Pen & Sword Books: After the Battle, Archaeology, Atlas, Aviation, Battleground, Discovery, Family History, History, Maritime, Military, Politics, Select, Transport, True Crime, Fiction, Frontline Books, Leo Cooper, Praetorian Press, Seaforth Publishing, Wharncliffe and White Owl.

For a complete list of Pen & Sword titles please contact

PEN & SWORD BOOKS LIMITED
George House, Beevor Street, Off Pontefract Road, Hoyle Mill, Barnsley,
South Yorkshire, England, S71 1HN.
E-mail: enquiries@pen-and-sword.co.uk
Website: www.pen-and-sword.co.uk

or

PEN AND SWORD BOOKS
1950 Lawrence Rd, Havertown, PA 19083, USA
E-mail: uspen-and-sword@casematepublishers.com
Website: www.penandswordbooks.com

CONTENTS

	Foreword	6
	Introduction	7
Chapter 1	1900s to 1939 – Motorhomes – The early beginnings	8
Chapter 2	Motorhomes gain popularity 1950–69	23
Chapter 3	The 1970s – The Motorhome's Highs and Lows	45
Chapter 4	1980 to 2000 Advances in Motorhome design and popularity	71
Chapter 5	2000–24	94

FOREWORD

The modern era has seen the motorhome become a leisure vehicle to which many aspire. The American dream of driving across states in a recreational vehicle brings up the feeling of freedom and discovering the open road. Motorhome owners feel like pioneers reaching out to seek new vistas and travelling in comfort. For those who don't realise, the motorhome discussed in this book is basically a caravan body built onto a chassis/cab.

The campervan is a conversion using a commercial van as its base, then adding interior fittings into the shell. The difference is that the campervan is more compact in size and therefore can go more off the beaten track and is a popular leisure vehicle today. Therefore, the two are quite different and also the motorhome is the older idea of the two. Using images from my archives and other sources, this book shows just how the motorhome has changed from a slow and unreliable vehicle to a sophisticated luxury hotel on wheels today.

Andrew Jenkinson

INTRODUCTION

This book is not an A-Z of motorhomes – for that you would need an enormous book! As in my *A Visual History Of Caravans* (Pen & Sword Transport, 2022), I have tried to include some lesser known makes that have played their part in the development of the modern motorhome. The motorhome didn't really take off in volume sales till the early 1960s, no doubt helped by the then Caravan Club eventually letting motorhome owners join the club in 1967. The 1970s saw more peaks and troughs and by the mid-1980s onwards, motorhomes were seen in increased numbers on UK roads and increasingly so in Europe. Motorhome sales have now reached new heights and look set to increase for years to come. But how did it begin? Who would make and market this new leisure vehicle?

This visual history of the motorhome allows the reader insight to the development of both the chassis/cab and the motorhome through carefully chosen images. Some may say that this was the golden era in motorhome history where accountants didn't have the final say on designs. It was also an era in the 1960s where base vehicles came from Ford, Bedford, Austin, Morris and Commer. The diesel engine wasn't employed, except for special customer orders. It was the petrol engine that was first choice, because it was cheap as well as having better overall performance.

The import explosion began with motorhomes from the United States and later into the 1980s European brands too. The new imported breed of chassis/cabs (including Japan) gave motorhome manufacturers greater scope in design and layouts. The 1970s boom in sales giving way to recession, while the motorhome today is again popular and aspired to leisure vehicle. This is then, the Visual History of the Motorhome.

1
1900s TO 1939 – MOTORHOMES – THE EARLY BEGINNINGS

There were a few ideas around pre-1919 on motorhome design, or as it was called the 'motorised caravan'. With the coming of the combustion engine, the idea of using this form of transport for mobile living accommodation was to be tried out by a few eccentric folk in the early 1900s. Some of these pioneers did not produce a caravan-bodied motorised unit on a commercial basis. This wasn't to happen till 1918 by a company in the UK – Eccles Motor Caravans at Gosta Green near Birmingham. The father and son Riley team had in fact designed their first motorised caravan in 1913, converting a Talbot touring car with a body added to make into sleeping accommodation.

The Eccles motorhome was built in the garage at their home with help from the gardener they employed. There were very few other motorised caravans around and these were built to special order. Some would never be recorded, i.e. photographed or any written information logged. In France there were a few prototype one offs and the US was home to some very outlandish designs. The trailer caravan at first was very primitive and the horse drawn caravan was still very much to the fore but that would change with the event of the First World War in 1914.

The Rileys had taken over the Eccles Motor Transport company after the war and after making prototype caravans and motorhome and displaying them at the 1919 Motor Show, selling the motorhome first. The Eccles Motor Caravan Co was born, with hard work undertaken to market the idea. The first commercial production of the motorhome had begun. Taking a big risk financially, the Rileys had to upgrade the premises as well as design, build, and promote their caravan and motorhome manufacturing business.

But it was the commercial builders who would be the ones to develop the motorhome, though many were built to order and for this we return to the Rileys. With the Eccles brand now dropping its transport section, its Gosta Green premises was committed to producing car pulled caravans, luxury showman caravans and the successful motorhome. Bill Riley junior worked hard to market the motorhome and the first one they had sold was in 1920 to Lady Rhondda who took to the Eccles motorhome and caused great publicity for it.

Eccles also introduced the motorhome idea to companies such as Philips and Exide as well as various organisations. The Eccles was a basic design that was then altered to suit the buyer's requirements. As time rolled on, other makers set up copying Eccles designs and after the Second World War there would be new developments in base vehicles as the beginning of the 1950s would be the opening for a new explosion in motorhome interest.

First motorhome produced by father and son team Bill Riley senor and Bill Riley junior in 1913/14 in their back garden outhouse. Helped by their gardener, they used a Talbot chassis and wrote about their 'motorised caravan' to the leading car journal *Autocar*. It was seen by a local coachbuilder who was set to make this motorised caravan under licence. With the outbreak of the First World War the idea was put on hold.

1906 and a special build for J.W. Mallalieu who lived in Wavertree, Liverpool. It wasn't the first motorhome in the country but one which attracted much attention with its lavish interior. Built on a Manchester company's Belsize chassis, the Mallalieu's motorhome was heavy and slow with just a 40hp engine. The Caravan Club's founder J. Harris Stone was impressed especially with the wine storage. With 4,072 kgs of weight the luxury motorhome always had to park on hard standing!

An Eccles motorcaravan based on a Morris chassis.

After the First World War, the Riley's bought the Eccles Transport Company based at Gosta Green Birmingham. They kept the owner on a Mr Eccles to run the transport while they went back to motorised caravans as well as trailers. The early 1920s Eccles motorhome parked outside the premises was to be produced in many guises throughout the decade. The Morris Chassis was used for this model pictured, but Fords and others were too. The Riley's designed/built and marketed the motorhome making it a commercial venture.

Norman Wilkinson-Cox was another early UK motorhome manufacturer. This 1928 Raven model was typical of the few they produced; they tended to build caravans but boasted they could build a coach-built body onto most brand's chassis especially using the Ford model T used here. For its period this was a good-looking motorhome. Raven again would go to trailer caravan production but for a few years made coach-built motorhomes. Raven made their name with caravans and also living caravans in the early 1950s.

1900s TO 1939 – MOTORHOMES – THE EARLY BEGINNINGS

Another angle of the Raven motorhome; note its simple lines and slightly curved front roof. Also, the cab was part of the actual living area of the motorhome; making it an early A class type design. Also look at the spoke front wheels and disc type one fitted at the rear. These features mentioned made the Raven distinctive from the Eccles models of the time.

Home built motorhomes were quite a thing; this was a home build but with an ingenious idea. The actual coach built caravan section could be taken apart and stored away in a garage. The lorry chassis was then free to do what it was designed to; the owner of the caravan body used to borrow a chassis to pop his caravan body bit back on! Once the holiday was over, he returned the lorry chassis!

Another cruder pair of home builds are in use here. Notice entrance doors copied the old caravan idea of a rear door. The facing motorhome is heavily jacked up at the rear of the axle line with bricks of some sort. Most of these home builds were made using old running gear as well as being at times looking very poorly put together.

A mid-1920s motorhome owned and designed by Mr Appleton; this was quite a compact design compared to some of the larger types. It also had a wraparound canopy which gave the 3m length motorhome the look of an aeroplane, a nickname given to it by those who saw it. Lightweight and compact for the day, J. Harris Stone was said to be impressed by its ability to get more off the beaten track than other motorhome designs.

Home built motorhomes varied in what chassis they used. In this 1927 built example, the owner used an old Standard car chassis adapted by a local blacksmith for the extra length. The family who owned it got involved with its build which took a year to complete. They travelled the UK exploring and it was still in use till the outbreak of the Second World War, when it was then used for war work. Home built designs often stayed in the family for years.

The Rileys' Eccles company was expanding its motorhome side; one market sector they created through this was to build specials for various companies and societies. Using a standard design, Eccles would customise the model to the buyer's requirements. This late 1920s unit for the Anti-Vivisection Society had a rear boarding step and also two wind down rear stabilisers.

Eccles design and development in motorhomes in the 1920s outshone the competition that was around back then. Using such chassis as a Ford, compact motorhomes such as this No 10 model were sold to garages for hiring out. Many sales were created by this hire market – note the neat build and design for which Eccles became known.

Another Eccles special, based on the mid-1920s Eccles No.10 model. This principle paid off in sales when the special was parked up in a town or city. People would ask about the vehicle and ask for details of the model – Eccles sold their motorhomes through this type of PR. Unfortunately, the image had no record of for whom the special was built!

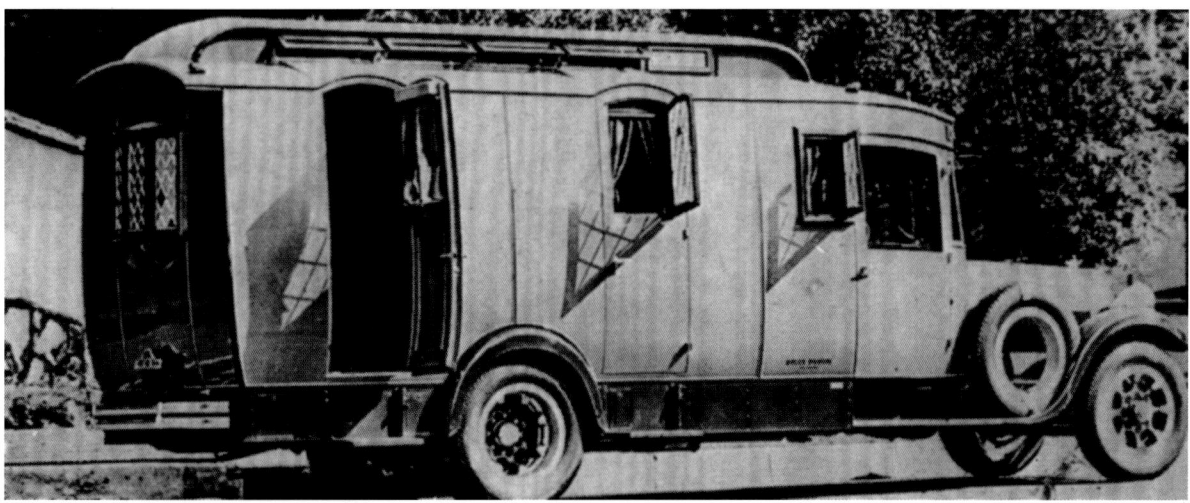

Made and designed by Melville Hart, a one-time Naval architect, the Flat van was a luxury motorhome that boasted an interior that appealed to well off buyers such as royalty. Based at St Stephens House on the Victoria Embankment the works were close to people with money. This 1924 version was one of several made with many of Hart's models being photographed outside Buckingham palace, no less. There were several models; this one pictured featured electric lighting and luxury fittings.

THE LIGHT CRUISER

Streamlined motorhomes of the 1920s did not come more so than the Road Yacht's Limited design Light Cruiser. Based on a standard chassis with 20hp engine on a 4m length body, it was designed as an easy to drive well equipped motorhome that encompassed the cab into the main bodywork. It had an on-board gramophone and electric lighting plus a lavatory and shower bath. Priced at £490 it was expensive but was an innovative design.

As most early caravan manufacturers did, Winchester luxury caravan builders also dipped their toe into the motorhome market in the 1920s. Building a few motorhomes, one notable model was based on the 1930 Streamlined touring caravan. In fact, basically it was the caravan which was mounted onto a lorry chassis. The caravan body incorporated the driving cab, but few were made and Winchester concentrated on caravans.

Jennings of Sandbach in Cheshire had built their first motorhomes from the late 1920s into the 1930s. They also built trailer caravans but the motorhome was to become their main source of manufacture. Making specials such as this for the British Ilse Gospel group, their coach building skills and quality finish would see Jennings become well known by the mid 1960s using Ford's popular Transits chassis cabs. Truck-maker ERF would become the owner of Jennings motorhomes by the 1970s.

Eccles were ahead of the game with designs and marketing of their motorhomes. They built all types of specials in the 1920s and early 1930s using all types of ideas and one was this extending rear floor with roof. This idea had been used notably on the early tent manufacturers Piggots first 1920s caravans but Jennings had also come up with this idea too, but it wasn't a design feature that proved successful.

Another Melville Hart hand-built luxury special motorhome, Hart also built caravans to order to. With customers' demands catered for where needed with many coming from overseas. This motorhome was a special for the Maharajah of Gwalior and was actually inspected by King George V and Queen Mary. Hart named his motorhomes Flat Vans, a name which become well known among the rich. Hart's Company would design matching caravans for the customer's motorhome to tow but the company only had a few years' short run before it closed down.

This late 1920s motorhome was quite compact and belonged to a Mr Appleton. In the early Caravan Club days Appleton's motorhome was popular on club meets, impressing caravan owning members with its lightweight and compact dimensions. With its pull-out side awnings, it looked like an aeroplane and was given that nickname. Appleton had designed it after several ideas and using his experience as a camper, though, sadly, no maker took the design to make on a commercial scale.

This is an example of an Eccles coachbuilt Caravan 19ft. long on Bedford six-wheel chassis.

Eccles Motorised Caravans – as they marketed them – were the leaders and included six-wheeler tag axle designs such as this on Bedford lorry chassis. The 'Molly Croft' or lantern roof was still a strong feature and though practical with helping improve ventilation it was also seen as a fashion styling feature to carried on over from the trailer caravans they built. This model dates from the late 1920s and would sleep four,

1900s TO 1939 – MOTORHOMES – THE EARLY BEGINNINGS

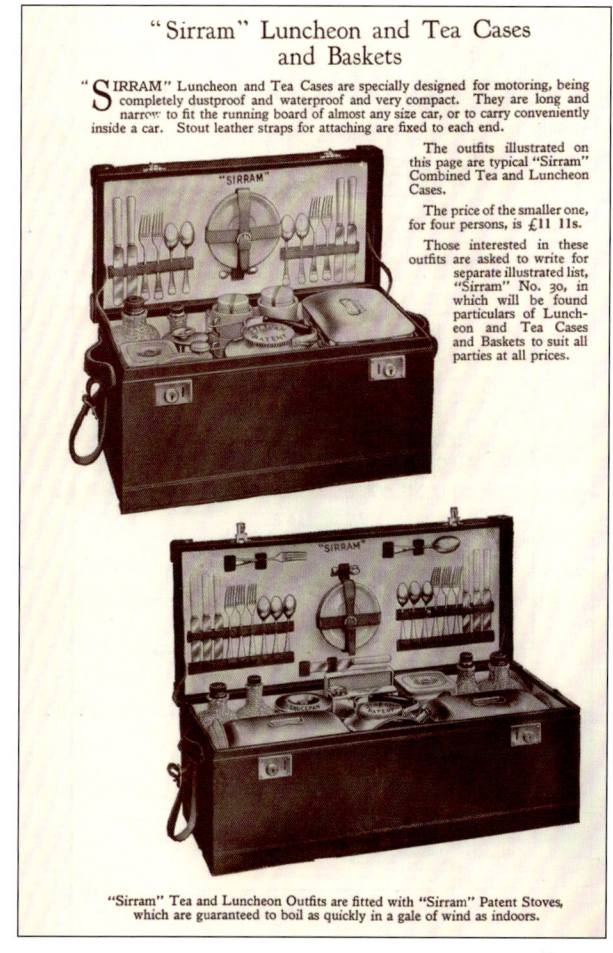

RIGHT: Sirram luncheon/tea baskets were very popular for the motorist. This self-contained package sold for nearly £12, a lot of money back then! Also these were aimed at the motorhome user, being ideal for those on the road between destinations. This brand was an upmarket basket and proved popular with motorhome owners.

BELOW: Eccles was able to make their motorhomes to customers' specifications such as this one for the Anglo Catholic Congress who had obviously seen the motorhome as an ideal mobile base for them. Such was Eccles' reputation in this infant industry that they were often first choice for many due to their quality and design features. The caravan makers who used one of their models and built onto a chassis found fewer buyers. Eccles designed motorhomes from the ground up.

The Covered Wagon Co, an American firm in the late 1930s, produced this then modern design. This motorhome was imported by Nomad Caravans, but few were sold here. The styling was very modern and showed the 1930s slant to aerodynamic modern styling. The lantern roof was still a feature – the design could have come from the late 1950s such were its modern overtones – and interiors would have been well appointed.

Motorhomes from this period had been using old lorry chassis or car chassis, on home builds especially. From the early motorhome designs, lorry chassis was the natural solution for a base vehicle, but the ride was often hard and shook the interior, breaking ornaments. From the 1930s, the coach chassis was seen as the answer, with softer ride and a quieter experience on the road. However, the trailer caravan was being chosen over the motorhome.

1900s TO 1939 – MOTORHOMES – THE EARLY BEGINNINGS 21

An Eccles motorhome special around late 1920s – this side of the business proved very profitable with existing designs such as this being used. Kitchens were often equipped with crockery and for heating oil stoves were used. Electric 12-volt lights for night illumination were also fitted but with the trailer caravan taking more production space up, Eccles slowed motorhome production down. More factory space for caravans was badly needed and so only special motorhomes would be built by the late 1930s.

By the mid to late 1930s, another war was looming, Eccles as ever were ahead and began designing mobile battlefield HQs as well as ambulances. They also looked at mobile hospital treatment units, using their motorhome experience in design but now using more modern lorry bases. By 1939, Eccles were receiving orders from all of the armed forces for these field mobile hospital units. Eccles would receive large orders in this period; their early years of struggle had paid off!

Although there were small concerns making motorhomes more to order, Eccles' progression from their early start to market and manufacture had seen the company become the name in trailer caravans and motorhomes. This advert showed just how the purpose-built factory in Stirchley Birmingham could, with its skilled workforce, produce several types of leisure vehicles. Note how it is still named 'Eccles Motor Caravans Ltd'.

A late 1920s, early 1930s six-wheeler motorhome, classed today as an A class, with the cab being encompassed into the coachwork. This could have been a special made for a wealthy customer – many took their motorhomes on adventure trips abroad, often writing in the press about their experiences and bringing back some artefact they had found on their travels. Many travelled to far-flung areas of the globe.

2
MOTORHOMES GAIN POPULARITY 1950-69

With the Second World War, caravanning had come to s stop and what motorhomes were around were generally taken by the government for war work. Stories abound of some luxury motorhomes being stripped for medical use and also other reports witnessed seats being fitted and the interiors ripped out so that soldiers could be transported. Some of these motorhomes that came back after the war were not usable for sleeping in and many were just scrapped. Some survived and were repaired to be used in the late 1940s. The war had seen generals such as Montgomery have a mobile headquarters, most likely an Eccles design and manufacture. There were several used in the war by generals on both sides such was the usefulness of the motorhome converted as offices with sleeping accommodation.

Changes in vehicle designs were on their way after the war and this would unexpectedly do two things – begin the campervan market and at the same time create a new motorhome industry, although very small. In 1950, Volkswagen had been rebuilt after being flattened during the war. VW at this time launched its new Microbus; a rear engined vehicle, the Type 2 as it was also called was used to carry goods without the need of a larger vehicle.

The VW Microbus was a vehicle that the German maker Westfalia Caravans saw as potential to convert for sleeping purposes. By 1951 they did the first VW Microbus conversion which was to be the pioneer of the campervan leisure vehicle. Named the camping box, this vehicle slowly was seen as an alternative to towing a caravan. In the UK, the VW attracted some attention but the new van conversion was not a caravan or car, leaving a grey area with the law. A van was exempt of the old purchase tax, but with windows in it was classed as a car, but because it had cooking facilities and sleeping accommodation it was seen as a caravan which were exempt.

This new VW vehicle was seen as ideal for tradesmen who didn't need a large vehicle but still one bigger than an estate car. The new van design was soon taken up by other manufacturers in the UK. Bedford launched their CA model, with slide side entrance. A refugee after the war, Peter Pitt saw the VW conversion and then did his own in 1956. This was followed by Maurice Calthorpe with his small business of converting this new breed of 764kg vans coming onto the market. His Home Cruiser, as did Pitt's VW, came with a mechanical raising roof design.

Campervans need to be mentioned because they played their part in the development of the motorhome. Morris brought out their J Series vans which were used for all sorts of business and even the Post Office and soon Ford launched its Thames 400E in 1957 which could also be made available as a cab and chassis. Bedford, Morris and Commer did this, which made these designs ideal for building a caravan body on the back.

Campervans that were creating a new market, though, were subject to 30mph as a caravan speed limit and also purchase tax, this though was lobbied by Peter Pit who explained that the campervan should be exempt of this tax while also the speed limit was changed to make these conversions the same as cars so no 30 mph limit. This would help sales as folk liked the idea of being able to use the conversion for day to day use yet making ideal accommodation too.

But this new niche market was now supporting six known companies producing conversions and now using the Atlas van for converting. Although a new breed of user of these models was expanding, some potential buyers were put off with the compact dimensions. This was where the coachbuilt motorhome was to become a good choice for many wanting extra space. Central Garage of Bradford Yorkshire had been around since the 1920s at least, selling new cars and repairing them. Into the 1950s, the company had a coach building and commercial vehicle department. In a quiet period, the director in charge of this division, Clifford Hobson, was looking at ways to keep his workforce occupied.

He decided on a project which was not a van conversion to a campervan, but a caravan constructed body on the back of a chassis cab – a Morris Commercial/Austin 152 chassis – in late 1957. Hobson had been involved in cabin cruiser boat designing and this put him in good stead for the project. In fact, all the team involved had ideas added; even the office secretary advised on soft furnishings! The quality was top notch, with ash-built body framework and mahogany furniture. Specification was impressive, with large fresh water and waste tank plus heater and full cooker. It cost around £1,200 so was aimed at the enthusiast. It also had a rear entrance door, a front dinette plus a toilet compartment and it slept up to four people. The brand name Paralanian was chosen and was taken from the works where the new motorhomes were produced, Parry Lane.

This new motorhome was shown at the 1958 Motor Show at Earls Court (caravans and motorhomes joined with car manufacturers) where it was successful and would inspire another company to produce something on the same lines but with a far cheaper price tag. Bluebird, the big Parkstone Caravan maker and also commercial van producer, saw the Paralanian, liked the idea and designed a similar design also using the Austin 152, and created the Bluebird Highwayman at £870 – a great deal cheaper than the Yorkshire hand-crafted Paralanian. The Bluebird Highwayman was the start of a motorised division for the company, making them popular and great value.

Although the van conversions were gaining popularity, especially with the VW microbus and the Ford Thames the rise of builders of coachbuilt models was also steady in gaining buyers. With this rise in both camps, the two main clubs the Camping Club (later the Camping and Caravanning Club) had allowed the few motorhome owners into their club with caravans. But motorhome and van conversion users were seen as a separate idea to the Club's ideals. They did accept them but had limitations set in place. Things were no better at the Caravan Club. Back then, members were very much involved and a hostile reaction towards motorhomes saw the Club ban them.

With both clubs seeing the motorhome as inferior (though the motorhome had been around longer than the touring caravan), motorhome owners needed an organization and on 17 January 1960, the Motor Caravanners Club was formed. It would be 1967 that the Caravan Club admitted motorhomes and van conversions, though at first they were not allowed on rallies!

A dedicated show at Earls Court for touring caravan, static caravan and park home manufacturers also would benefit the new small wave of motorhome makers appearing. This opened up the caravan industry for both tourers, statics and park home manufacturers, but also for the few convertors and motorhome makers. The Earls Court Show was the show for many years where buyers from abroad came and would place large orders for exports. Over the years there would be regional dealer-held shows with caravans, tents and motorhomes and campervans. These shows would attract a large audience and dealers would find them lucrative for attracting new customers. Over the years there would be special motorhome and campervan combined shows and an increasing number of regional shows in places such as Leeds, Manchester and Glasgow.

Dormobile had, like others, been involved with using glass fibre mouldings but they were to take things a step further. Their Debonair model in 1964 was a classic in the making with the GRP body shell based on a Bedford CA. The intense manufacturing process meant that this first Dormobile Coachbuilt was not easy to mass produce. Using a giant mould for the body, the process meant that after it came out of the mould, it needed finishing off before being then fitted to the chassis cab. The Debonair did look an attractive unit adding to the Dormobile success. It had clean lines for the time and had a unique two room layout. To help keep costs down, the Debonair shared some GRP moulds with an ambulance/minibus that the company produced, but it was still a labour-intensive job to build.

Dormobile would become an almost generic name or the campervan – people calling a campervan a Dormobile when it was possibly a Devon or Danbury conversion. Adding to the Debonair's success a few years later, Dormobile added a new coachbuilt named the Land Cruiser at the 1966 Earls Court Caravan Show. The Dormobile design team combined the GRP moulds they had used with the Debonair and went for the Leyland 20 as its base, surprisingly not using the Bedford CA as for the Debonair. Though by the next decade, Dormobile would swap over to the new Bedford CF.

One family who helped to bring the motorhome to the fore was the Johnson family in 1965. The Johnsons, with their two children, set off on a 60,000 mile round the world tour with their Bluebird Highwayman and finally came back to the UK in 1968, praising the Highwayman's rugged build and comfort levels. The Highwayman had become the biggest selling coach built in the UK and with the Bluebird and Sprite merger in 1963 had given the Ci Group immense buying power which enabled them to also have a large budget for marketing which back then saw them advertising in all the major car/caravan related magazines.

After Bluebird had merged with Sprite/Eccles caravans, the Caravans international group expanded quickly, with the Bluebird motorised division having London based Crofton Garages become sole dealers. Ci soon made an offer and took over the Crofton business. There were a few makers who would also design a motorhome for and build it to a dealership's specification. With the advent of Ford replacing the Thames van with the new Transit in 1965, Ford had been influenced by the mass take up of vans conversions but also the growing number of coach-built motorhomes. The Transit was bigger and better than the Thames and makers such as Jennings coachbuilders saw the Transit as an ideal base for larger coach-built designs. New engines for more power were developed by Ford for the larger Transits, including a 1.7 litre and 2 litres, both petrol of course.

The 1960s had indeed been a decade of growth in motorhomes and many smaller concerns would get overlooked with short production runs and few dealers. The caravan movement had in the mid 1950s formed a rallying event, testing drivers and caravans to the limit. By the next decade, the motorhome would also be allowed to take part in this yearly event organised by the Caravan Club, though motorhome manufacturers were not seen in numbers like the caravan industry.

With the increase in sales of motorhomes, the accessory market was also growing and one of the items seen as a must by some motorhome owners was the addition of the awning. These could be supplied to add onto the motorhome or work as a frame tent so kept separate and left on site making your pitch safe from anybody just pitching on because the motorhome user wasn't there. Some owners would put a bucket over the pitch number to say this is a pitch that isn't vacant. Some owners made their own signs with such things written on them saying don't pitch here – it's ours and Motorhome only here.

We come to the end of this chapter to see a mini boom for 1970, also the motorhome was becoming very popular and for those who didn't want to splash out on a new motorhome, you could in effect make your own. Quite a few did, but others also had specials built by local coach building firms or some caravan makers such as Creighton, based in Accrington. In that period most companies would produce a motorhome for customers as one offs or some companies such as Dandy Caravans near Wigan tried to diversify. Dandy had in the late 1960s begun to build camping trailers that folded out for site use. The company was no doubt influenced by the Mongoose Mini based motorhome decided to make their version.

They built a conversion with a simple layout of a dinette cooker and sink – the idea was to get sales in this expanding market to run alongside the camping trailers. When the venture didn't take off, the company then looked at a coach-built motorhome using the Rootes Commer chassis and a steel framework instead of the usual wooden one. However Dandy would not produce this design till the next decade.. The motorhome market was strong as the motorhome was discovered by more people who looked at this leisure vehicle having more kudos than the caravan.

The movement was seen by many as a great lifestyle and with big dealerships such as Wilsons and also up-and-coming Turners. while in the north, Madison's Motor Caravans were expanding. Having begun in the 1960's near Southport, Madison's would by the next decade move to a new and much larger premises near Kirkham on the outskirts of Blackpool and Preston.

One thing that the coach-built motorhome market didn't witness much was actual home-built DIY designs that were quite common in the delivery van sector. Producing a coach-built motorhome was a job for those who were not only very good at woodworking skills such as a joiner, but also had a workshop in which to build it. The van conversions were an easier task with mainly the adding of a window, the rest being the furniture fitted inside. However, at one stage and this may by today's standards sound odd, some people would look out for old coach-built ambulances that came up for sale.

The idea of using such a vehicle was deemed as a good idea in the 1960s and into the 1970s too. Bought relatively cheaply and with some miles left in them, some DIYers could convert them into some quite attractive units. Others, though, looked still like an ambulance with a caravan-like interior. Some owners kept the blacked-out side windows too! Campsites readily allowed them on, knowing that these were a home-built conversion, some great and others not so great! The other option for the aspiring motorhome DIYer was the possibility of a commercial coach-built van being bought. This was an idea that again meant that adding a window or two was needed on the bodywork and a paint job then fitting in the furniture.

The DIY idea does continue in modern times and again it is mainly down to vans being bought cheaply then kitted out. The motorhome, though, was to make great strides and even though a recession hit, the motorhome industry would ride the storms though not without some casualties on the way. The new vehicle bases from such as Toyota would encourage more new motorhome builders to the marketplace but also Leyland's Sherpa would become a popular choice for motorhome manufacturers.

MOTORHOMES GAIN POPULARITY 1950–69

There would be a Hull based major caravan manufacturer A-Line Caravans who would join the motorhome market in 1975, thus proving that the motorhome was selling in greater numbers. Over the coming years more caravan manufacturers would add motorhome's to their portfolio. It was reputed that 15,000 motorhomes were being sold by the late 1970's, though accurate figures weren't available but it showed how the motorhome market had grown since the 1960's.

More dealerships would join in, taking a franchise on of a motorhome manufacturer and the then Auto Sleeper brand that had been a convertor also launched its new coach-built along with Richard Holdsworth another early campervan maker also went into coach-built motorhomes. The motorhome was a good proposition for those in entertainment as well as sports people.

All that was going on the 1960s had given the coach-built motorhome market good firm foundations and as always with any industry some of the early makers would for whatever reason fall by the wayside or just drop out of the market to concentrate on other projects. So there were going to be highs and some lows in the decade of the 1970s and some new ideas of how to attract caravanners to coach-built motorhome ownership.

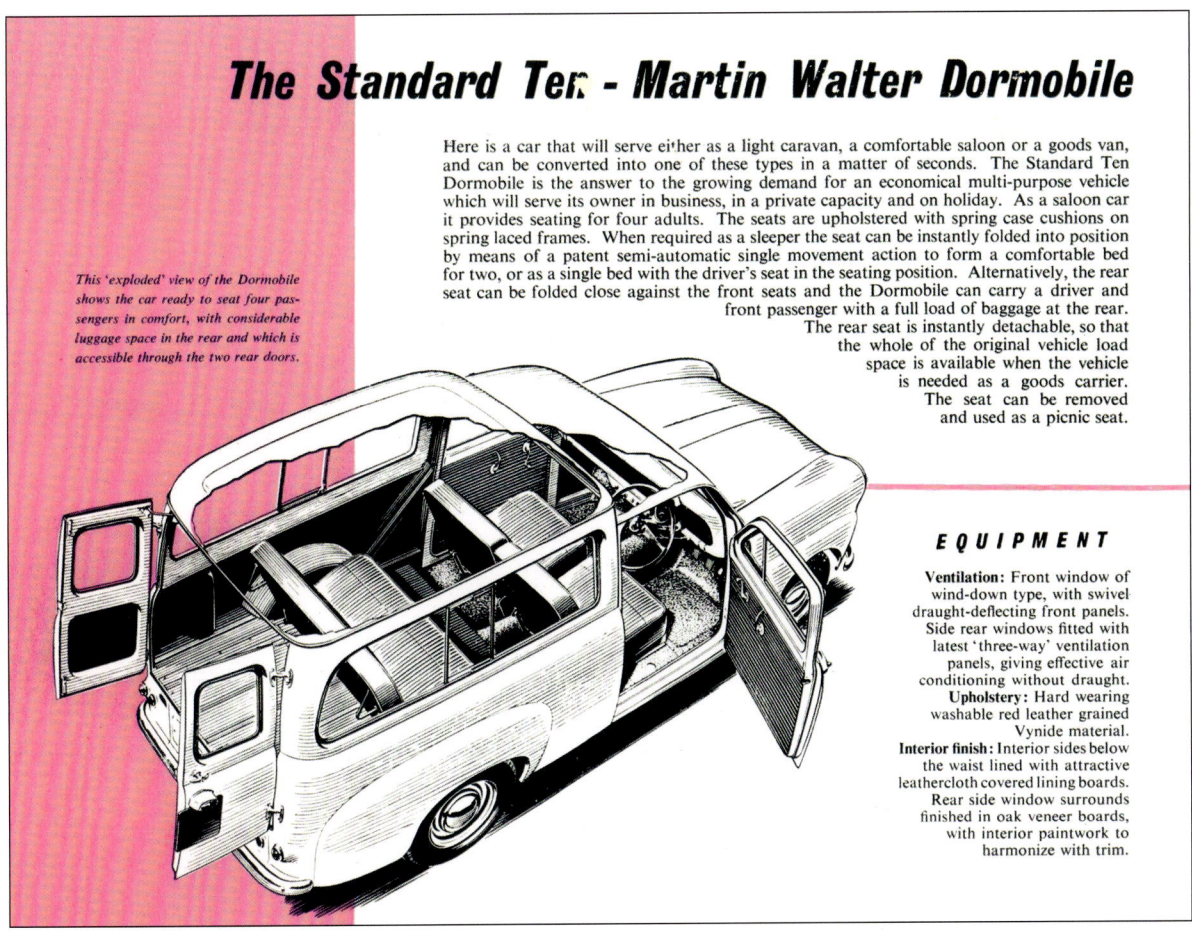

The name Dormobile would become the household name in the UK for campervans and motorhomes. Martin Walter was a coachbuilder for many years and had become van convertors. This Standard Ten (pictured) was a conversion to a basic campervan after an employee of the Kent based company noted people sleeping in their car to catch the early ferries. Dormobile was the name given to this basic design making a double bed in the Standard Ten.

ABOVE: As the new lightweight delivery vans emerged in the 1950s, Dormobile designed a campervan conversion on VW, Ford Thames and Bedford CA, making then a top producer. Dormobile were clever with their designs and other convertors followed their ideas. The elevating roof with candy pattern design became a Dormobile trademark. By the 1960s, Dormobile had expanded their range to include a new coach-built model in 1964 named the Debonair. Although better known for their conversions, they did develop more coach-built models.

OPPOSITE ABOVE: The late 1950s would witness a new flow of motorhome manufacturers, some producing just a few units before they stopped production. One was Summerdale, a caravan manufacturer near Blackpool making both tourers and holiday caravans. Built on a Bedford CA chassis cab, the Summerdale had been designed to include the cab making it what we would call today an A Class motorhome. The lines were flowing and was typical 1950s in style – the Summerdale was a two berth with end lounge area, but few were built.

OPPOSITE BELOW: The Paralanian was made when Central Garage sales in Bradford were slack. In charge of the repair division, Clifford Hobson, who had designed cabin cruisers, saw the increasing interest in campervans. In 1957, his division built a coach-built motorhome naming it the Paralanian – showing it at the 1957 Motor Show. Its design and caravan-like interior design proved popular, with sales taken. Based on an Austin chassis cab, it inspired Bill Knott of Bluebird Caravans and they built a similar design named Highwayman, but with fewer frills and at a cheaper cost.

MOTORHOMES GAIN POPULARITY 1950–69   29

Sprite Caravans headed by Sam Alper OBE were innovative in many ways; perhaps not one of their best ideas, this Pic-a-Bac Cabin dropped onto a pick-up like the Land Rover. It slept two, had a dinette and side split kitchen and the cost was around the £157 mark. To remove it, you had to get four people to stand at each corner and lift off/on the back of the pick-up. It was a cross between a motorhome and caravan, but it never made production.

OPPOSITE ABOVE: Using the Austin J2, this was Bluebird's Highwayman coach-built motorhome from 1958. Sharing similar design to the Paralanian which Knott had seen in 1957, he wanted to build a more affordable coach-built using Bluebird's resources from horse box/box delivery vans they produced. The Highwayman was to sell very well over the years being obviously modernised in that period. Bluebird's Highwayman slept four and was on a Morris J2 with 42bhp engine. It came with a 22-litre water tank, gas hob/sink and also a large 1.78 m x 0.58 m central Perspex roof vent at £800.

OPPOSITE BELOW: A cut-away of the Morris/Austin BMC chassis, this was ideal for the coachbuilder when launched, becoming a standard platform for several motorhome builders. The van version was popular with campervan builders too. It was a well-known vehicle and was used for many different purposes, though the motorhome manufacturer proved to be a strong customer for it. The engine was a 1.5 petrol, but no MPG figures were available; driven steadily, it would be possible to get around 28 mpg.

MOTORHOMES GAIN POPULARITY 1950–69

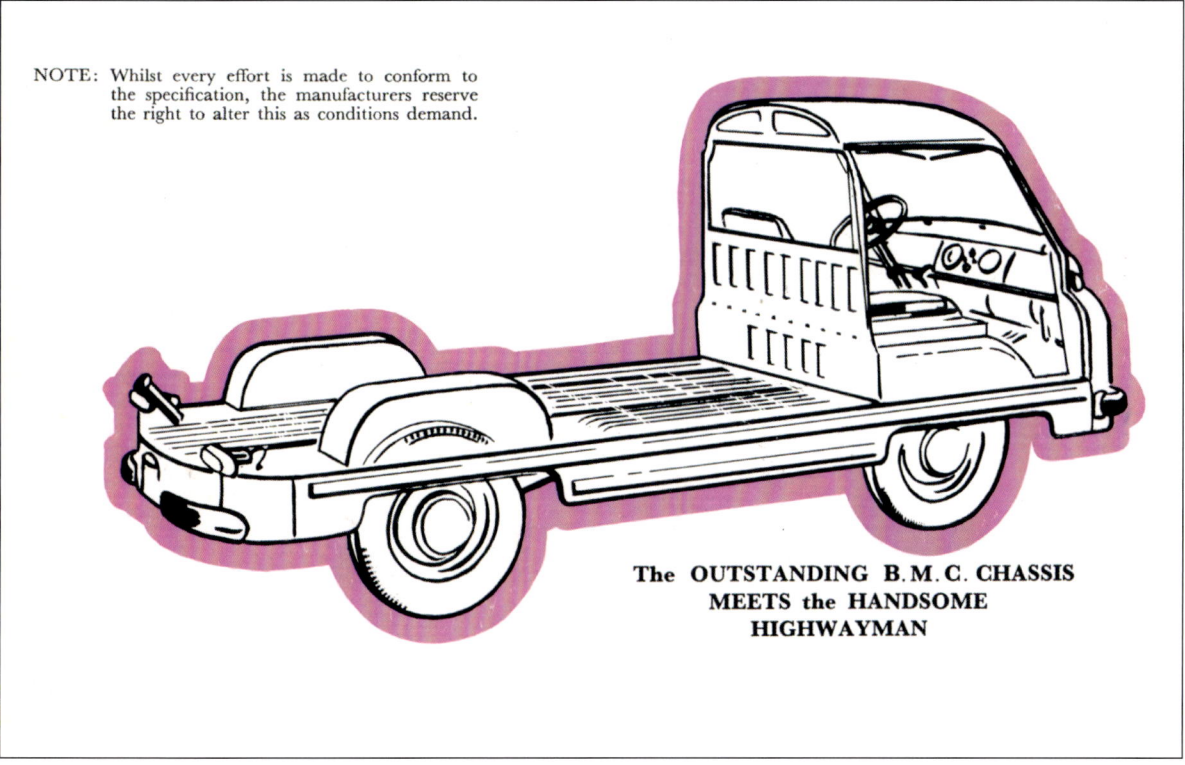

NOTE: Whilst every effort is made to conform to the specification, the manufacturers reserve the right to alter this as conditions demand.

The OUTSTANDING B.M.C. CHASSIS MEETS the HANDSOME HIGHWAYMAN

ABOVE: Built near Newcastle, this deluxe early 1960s Hadrian coach-built motorhome produced several models in its line up. This luxury model here was an early model based on the Ford Thames. Hadrian designed some excellent practical end kitchen layouts which became a feature of the brand. Hadrian used the BMC Austin 152/Morris J2, and Bedford CA. The Hadrian came with a cold storage locker, cooker, storage water tank, 12-volt lights and even a chemical loo; by the end of the decade Hadrian had ceased production.

OPPOSITE ABOVE: Cotswold was another luxury maker – sold by Ken Stephens Caravans near Gloucester. This 1965 Series C was another luxury motorhome using the popular Austin 152. Using aluminium and GRP panels, the brand soon got a following from those wanting luxury, well-built motorhomes with conversions later carried out on Mercedes lorry bases and also using the ever-popular Ford Transit. Cotswold Series C had a rear lounge dinette and front L-shaped kitchen area with lavatory next to it in the front corner.

OPPOSITE BELOW: By 1962, the Paralanian had a new profile, one which made it easy to spot on site and road. The design still used the rear end for the entrance, a feature that would be used for many years. An Austin 152 chassis cab was made to blend into the Paralanian styling while quality was key with excellent cabinet work and practical design. The Paralanian was one of the better known coachbuilts of this period along with Bluebird's Highwayman.

MOTORHOMES GAIN POPULARITY 1950–69

LEFT: Motorhome and campervan users were not at that time welcome in the two main clubs. The motorhome/campervan movement was growing and by June 1960 a club was formed just for motorhome and campervan owners. The Club was formed to also give the movement a voice. Within a few years, the club was firmly established with membership growing quickly. They produced their own magazine and got backing from manufacturers as well as dealers. Rallies were held and the club became influential in the trade as well as the public domain.

BELOW: As in any club, there has to be a sideline in club regalia and the Motor Caravanners Club owners were no exception. Badges for jackets and hats plus of course your motorhome and a pennant were all sold to members. Some of the items such as stickers and keyrings were free to new members. The club also had a stand at the caravan show at Earls Court, where members could stop for a tea or coffee.

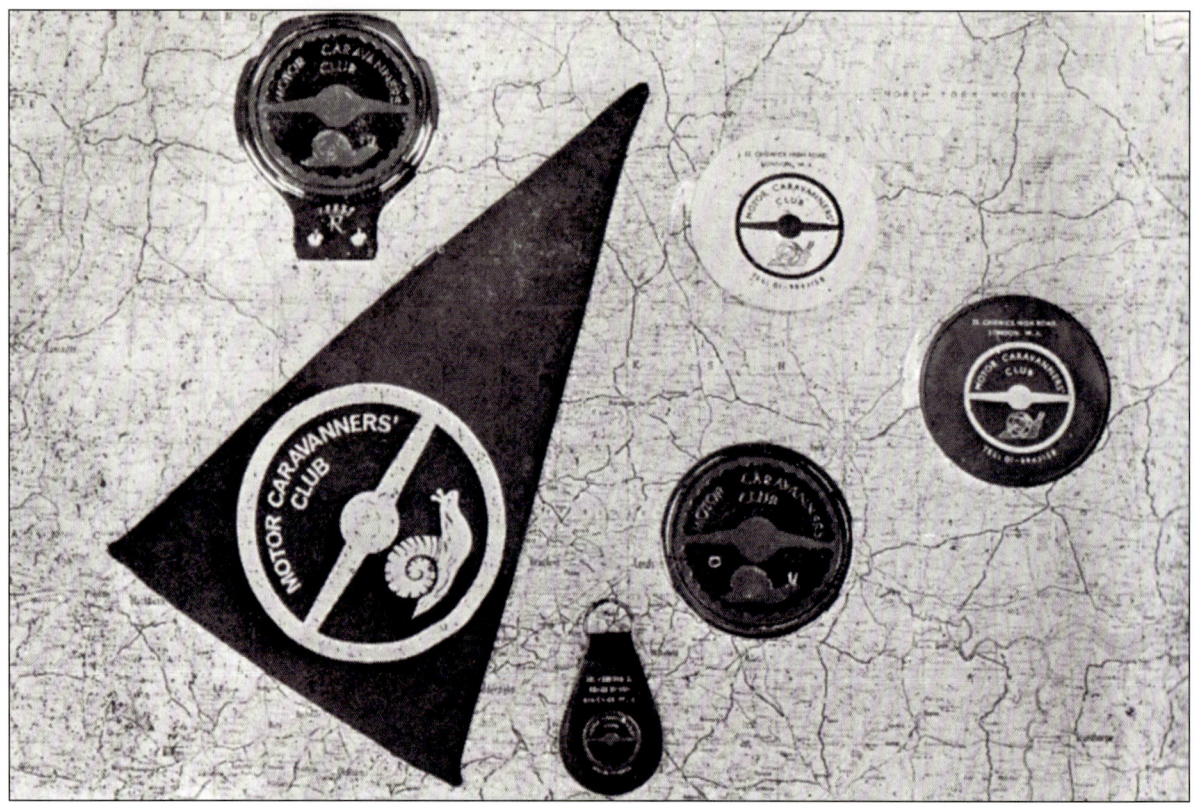

MOTORHOMES GAIN POPULARITY 1950–69

A de-commissioned Bedford coachbuilt ambulance – vehicles such as these could be bought cheaply, so the DIYer could fit out these vehicles as a cheap motorhome. From old delivery vans to ambulances, many wanted to come up with their own layouts/interiors. This period saw many old ambulances being bought and people fitting in a kitchen and seating. Seeing an old ambulance with curtains and maybe a revamped spray job wasn't uncommon on site and road in the 1960s!

There were still coachbuilders who would build specials such as this example. Based on a Commer, this mid-1966 coach-built was apparently built for owners who had a cat and a ladder was supplied so that the cats could come and go as they pleased! There were those customers who still wanted a special motorhome built and as the 1970s progressed, this niche market would fade away as more choice in motorhomes saw a wider availability in layout designs. *(Photo courtesy John Lunt)*

ABOVE: Creighton Binns were primarily caravan manufacturers in Nelson. The company also built cabin cruisers and mobile homes as well as tourers, but the company made a few coachbuilt motorhomes. From 1964/5, Creighton used Commer chassis cabs. Low production saw quality build, with real oak veneers. The company finished making caravans and also motorhomes. Creighton concentrated on making caravan-based layouts in the few motorhomes they built. *(Photo courtesy John Lunt)*

OPPOSITE ABOVE: Jennings returned to motorhome manufacture now under ERF trucks at Sandbach in Cheshire and in 1968 they used a LWB Land Rover for a coachbuilt conversion. The build was a special and was going to be used to tow a caravan as well. This 2-berth had the door put onto the side from the usual rear entry door. Jennings used Ford, Commer and BMC for their usual coach-built motorhomes, all named Road Rangers. Jennings had a small but loyal customer base, and they would build special custom models such as the Land Rover motorhome.

OPPOSITE BELOW: The BMC Mini was a hit with many motorists and an iconic car, from its variants the Mini van was looked at by several convertors but also coachbuilders. This named the Mongoose was a coach-built micro motorhome with extending vertical roof to enable head room when on a pitch. The Mongoose was built using a Mini van supplied by the customer who was then charged £455 for the coach-built conversion. Few Mongoose motorhomes were made by this small concern who also built a micro caravan based on their micro motorhome. Mongoose were one of many small concerns trying to carve a slice of the motorhome market for themselves.

MOTORHOMES GAIN POPULARITY 1950–69

CIM were the biggest motorhome manufacturers in the UK and were part of the Caravans International Group. In 1965, the Johnson family drove their Bluebird Highwayman around the world covering 80,000 miles – a great bit of PR for CIM division of Ci. The family arrived back three years later without much fuss (no social media in 1968!) they had the Commer base vehicle – but the family reported that the Highwayman proved rugged and reliable. Comfort for five was also scored highly!

The Bluebird Highwayman based on the Morris – by 1966 the design had changed with tweaks over the years. Two large side windows let in more natural light as well as more ventilation. The Highwayman was the best-selling motorhome in the UK and the company exported them into Europe and sold some further afield including Canada and America at one point. The Highwayman gave many the opportunity to afford a new motorhome and became a benchmark in the industry.

Jennings with another of their custom-built specials; this was built in 1968 on an Austin Princess Van Den Plas, photo taken in the 1990s. This is now owned by John Lunt and is a one off using the Road Ranger design. This had been specified keeping the entrance door at the rear. Jennings' craftsmanship was to become well known and they would build on most bases if it was viable to do so. Handling must have been quite an experience! *(Photo courtesy of John Lunt)*

Dormobile had been known for their quality coach building before converting vans in the 1950s. In 1964 they launched their first coachbuilt motorhome using the Bedford CA base. This 1967 Debonair model shows the GRP coachbuilt body and note the window area too – it was a classic in styling. The Debonair sold well and was only built on the Bedford CA and later the CF. Its distinctive profile was easy to spot on the road. The Formica finish on furniture made it a very 1960s interior.

One of the most unusual designs in motorhome history! Named the Cara-Boot, this Mini had a trailer section to it with the rear end coming away from the body. The roof extended and on top of this was a boat! This idea would be classed as a hybrid leisure vehicle now but the complicated production would make it expensive to market. So, not surprisingly, the Cara-Boot was a bit of a sales flop; it would be interesting if the concept would work better in today's market.

1969 Jennings Road Ranger was a superb crafted coach-built motorhome and its leanings were towards the Yorkshire built Paralanian which was not surprising because the Jennings Road Ranger was designed by an ex Paralanian employee. so it was easy to see the influence in the Road Rangers profile. Interiors were hand crafted with real wood veneers and storage was another feature. Jenning's kitchens were known for their practical design and spec that included a hob and full oven.

Sprite Motorhome

ABOVE: The Sprite coachbuilt Ford Transit-based motorhome was unlike its touring caravan counterpart in that it had a good specification including shower and oven and was a quality built unit. Launched for 1967, the Sprite motorhome was given a good overall review by the press with its good specification including an electric water pump and full oven. However, the Sprite badge meant cheap and cheerful not luxury and the sales were not good as buyers looked elsewhere. It ran for two seasons only, being discontinued in late 1969.

RIGHT: Dormobile were noted for their coach building skills and also would produce one-off coachbuilts such as this Commer based A Class or as called then a 'walk through'. Built for Mr Noyes, it was 6.7m in length and could sleep four as well as double up as an office. It had fridge, oven, heating, generator, 12 volt light system, extractor fans the list was endless for the mid 60s. It also, unusually, was insulated with polystyrene and not glass fibre.

The Americans would call this a 'family motor coach', but the Noyes motor caravan can also be used as an executive office.

Though an oven cooker, refrigerator, and wash basin are included, the feeling of spaciousness is not lost.

All-round visibility is a feature apparent in this photograph of the well-appointed interior.

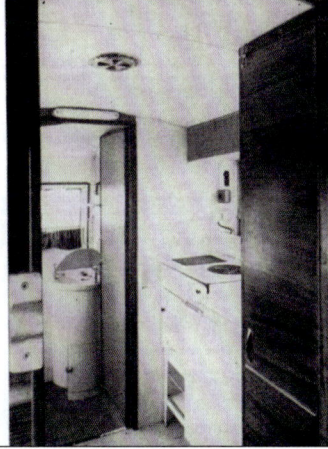

A VISUAL HISTORY OF MOTORHOMES: PHOTOGRAPHS FROM THE 20s TO MODERN DAY

This rare image is a Murray Caravan Co BMC Mini van coachbuilt conversion. This idea was one of a few to appear in this era. Around 1965/6, Murray thought this was the ideal micro motorhome for those on a budget and also short on parking space. It had a cooker and hand basin and could also have the optional clip-on toilet side tent for £7 extra! Murrays also looked at demountable units as well as a full blown coachbuilt. They also made trailer tents naming them Dandy Caravans.

Following the success of the Debonair coachbuilt motorhome, Dormobile launched the Land Cruiser for 1967. This time they used the Leyland 20 for its base; sleeping up to four, it cost around £1,400 and included two bedrooms. Using GRP, the Land Cruiser had much in common with the Debonair in sharing components. The Land Cruiser would also become as iconic as the Debonair, but it was the latter that many motorhome users remembered. A few years later it would use the Bedford CF as its new base vehicle.

MOTORHOMES GAIN POPULARITY 1950–69   43

RIGHT: Wilsons were to become the biggest motorhome and campervan dealers in Europe. The company had grown from the early 1900s as a car dealership and this family business had captured the early start of motorhomes. They held rallies and also were to open up several more dealerships. The company had expanded vastly in the 1960s and also had hiring fleets abroad and here in the UK. They were extremely prolific and also for a short while built their own luxury motorhomes.

BELOW: The Wilsons Group decided to build what we would call today an A - class motorhome. Leslie Wilson the owner wanted to make a luxury motorhome with a high specification included. Wilson thought a market for this luxury motorhome he named Adventurer existed. Built on a Commer chassis, this motorhome with all its fittings cost £3,000 but sales were poor and by the late 1960s was dropped. This Adventurer is outside the Wilson main dealership which is now a British Heart Foundation shop with flats above.

Dormobile was the brand that connected the general public with campervans and also motorhomes. This aerial view of the Folkestone factory shows just what a huge concern it had become by the end of the 1960s. Note all the Bedford CA vans lined up waiting to have conversions carried out. Dormobile looked unstoppable but changes in ownership, strong competition and some models which did not see much success witnessed the company fold by 1994.

3

THE 1970s – THE MOTORHOME'S HIGHS AND LOWS

This is a decade that rocked the nation as a whole. It all began well but soon problems arose with high inflation, a fuel crisis, a miners' strike, power cuts and the three day week; it all began to look that there was no end in sight. So, where would a poor economy leave the motorhome industry? Would this all become the end of such a promising start in the late 1950s? The decade began rather well. The fact that motorhomes were now getting more popular each year saw this market sector grow considerably.

The 1970s were also to witness the growing number of manufacturers cheating by putting a touring caravan body on the back of, say, a Ford Transit Custom and classing that as a motorhome, but more on those later. There was also a rise in the demountable coachbuilt body; an idea from America. Several small concerns entered this niche market area which was to be dominated by one brand; Suntrekker. Built by ICP, a division of dealers Southern Caravans, this new idea was launched in 1972 at the Earls Court Caravan Show. The Suntrekker was placed away from the main parts of the show, but word got about and soon during the show's duration visitors came to seek it out specially.

The idea was to use it with a vehicle such as a Ford Transit or Bedford CF pick up, so that it could be put onto the back quite easily. One of the problems was that the Suntrekker did not create much interior extra space over a conventional motorhome but also they did tend to rattle a lot when on the road. The build quality wasn't always the best from the Watford based factory. They came with a fridge and cooker plus a loo compartment and the sales, although never massive, were enough to keep the company producing these units. Some were sold abroad and ICP handed over to Walkers & Son, who developed more models to go onto different pick-up vehicles.

They were to be the leaders in this niche market with other small concerns also trying to grab their share. Murray Caravans (mentioned in the last chapter) who had produced a coachbuilt motorhome using the BMC minivan, had now gone on to making trailer tents and became successful in this market. However, proprietor Howard Murray designed a new coachbuilt using the Commer chassis cab in 1972. The design was simple, and few were made but renaming the company Dandy Caravans saw Dandy manufacture a pick up in 1972/3 named the Pic-A-Back. It slept three but was basic and based on the Eastern European Moskovich vehicle which was cheap to buy, so enabling the Dandy to come in at £975. But with their tent trailer sales, demand would see Dandy concentrate on that market dropping the motorhome idea.

The Caraboot launched by the Preston maker Mobile Holiday Units with its BMC Mini van half coachbuilt and detachable trailer section, released plans for a larger unit using the BMC Austin/Morris 1800 large saloon car. This time it was to use a complete GRP rear section with a type of Luton top design over the car's roof that would house a fixed double bed. An extra section for the coachbuilt construction was rigid and added another axle making it a six-wheeler. Cost and lack of sales saw possibly only a prototype built.

The end of the 1960s had seen around 3,000 campervans/motorhomes sold but by the early 1970s this had increased at 15,000 though figures were said not to be accurate. But with new motorhome makers coming, the expansion of dealers meant that more buyers could be reached. Big car dealers Godfrey Davis went into motorhomes, The Gailey Group, a large, growing company setting up dealerships, rapidly took on motorhomes by the mid-1970s. Other dealers grew and Wilson's, the longest established group, were also running hiring fleets at home and abroad. Turners were another expanding group along with Greens of Epping. Another new dealership named Marquis also was founded in 1973 and would expand its sales depots over the coming years.

THE 1970s – THE MOTORHOME'S HIGHS AND LOWS

OPPOSITE: ICP were part of one-time caravan dealers Southern Caravans; this American idea was not one that was successful in the UK. Launched in late 1972, the Suntrekker pick up was a crowd drawer. Most were exported and later Suntrekker was taken over by Walker Coachbuilders, then by the late 1970s the company sold the rights to Island Plastics. Cost was around £2,400 in 1973/4 and were designed to go on the Ford Transit/Bedford CF. A Trekker was entered in the once popular British Caravan Road Rally

BELOW: Ci Group was the biggest caravan manufacturer in the world in the 1970s. Their motorised division was also huge, with models such as the Landliner, a luxury motorhome using a 2 litre petrol engine Ford Transit. Note the space and the contemporary modern styling of this 1971 model. Part of the spec was a shower and a manual flush Porta Potti loo and low wattage strip lighting. The Ci motorised division had increased its sales from 700 in 1970 to 1,400 in 1971 as motorhome sales increased rapidly.

Wilsons not only sold motorhomes in the UK but also abroad and a large hiring out division, again to overseas customers. Wilsons had increased its sales grounds to four by 1973 and were the biggest motorhome (selling 2,000 units a year) dealership in the world. The company also sold cars and by the early 1980s the company moved to just selling cars and vans and no longer dealt with motorhomes. Wilsons still exist, but as a car dealership, still using the original logo, though!

The 1970s still witnessed home builds such as this splendid and distinctive looking coachbuilt using a lorry chassis. There was lots of panelled wood on the outside which would have taken time to maintain. Interior furniture in the lounge was all free standing so – mainly deckchairs! An L shaped kitchen was fitted with a fridge and twin burner hob with grill. It apparently took months to build – it was completed in 1971 and powered by a rather underpowered non-turbo diesel engine!

THE 1970s – THE MOTORHOME'S HIGHS AND LOWS

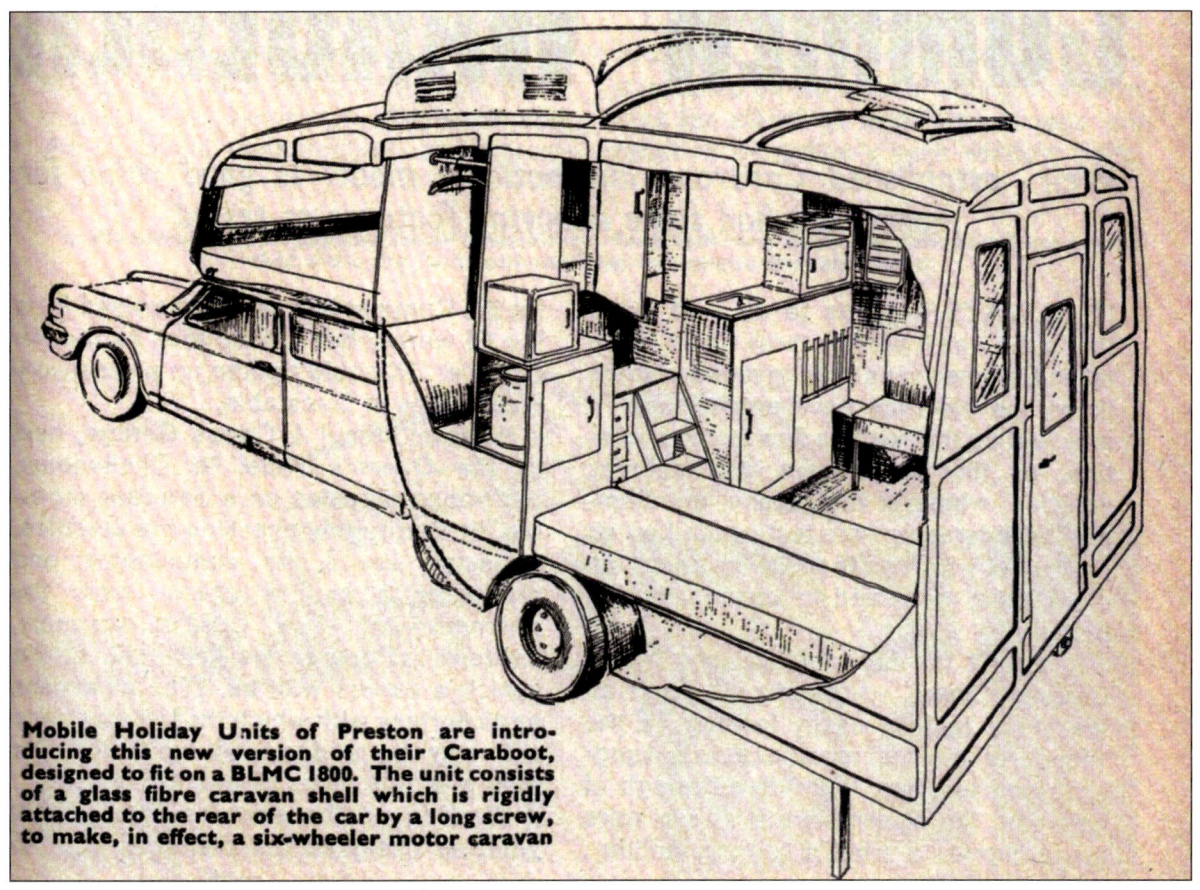

Mobile Holiday Units of Preston are introducing this new version of their Caraboot, designed to fit on a BLMC 1800. The unit consists of a glass fibre caravan shell which is rigidly attached to the rear of the car by a long screw, to make, in effect, a six-wheeler motor caravan

After the Caraboot BMC Mini coachbuilt a few years previously, the company, Mobile Holiday Units of Preston, designed a new GRP shell to fit the larger BMC Austin/Morris 1800 – this time an extra axle would be fitted to make it a six wheeler motorhome. The expense and production of this design meant that it never reached production, but its design was quite ingenious for 1971!

Sun-Tor were based in North Devon and began converting in 1968, mainly Austins to campervans. By the mid-1970s, they produced their first coachbuilt motorhome based on the recently launched Leyland Sherpa named Tor–Royal. It was a layout sleeping up to four with an overhead cab double bed. It was well equipped but Sun-Tor concentrated on its campervans, dropping the Sun-Tor coachbuilt. Sun-Tor would be taken over by Brownhills in 1980, concentrating on a Morris Ital conversion.

Looking dated in modern times, this Ford Transit based motorhome was the new 1971 Spacequest made in Cardiff by Thomas Hoskins and Sons. Costing £1,996, this motorhome came with shower/lavatory and hot and cold water plus an oven. Sleeping two, the lounge was at the front with split side kitchen and a rear corner washroom with wardrobe opposite. Entry was at the rear but could be closed off when the shower was being used and separate from the lounge, almost a rear end washroom.

The 1970s still would witness small coachbuilders build one off motorhomes, such as this one spotted on a motorhome rally in 1974. These types of builds were often not as stylish as the main manufacturer's of this vehicle, though this Bedford based special build was well finished off inside and out. This period would still see coachbuilders who were to get into this booming leisure vehicle market. *(Photo courtesy John Lunt)*

ABOVE: Auto-Kabin was another bespoke maker who built to order and their claim to fame was they did the first commercial pick-up design motorhome in the UK. They built on Mercedes, Ford, BMC or Commer but also a VW chassis cab could be ordered. This model slept three and had a large kitchen and also a spacious rear end lounge. The name, like many, disappeared in this decade. The Auto-Kabin was distinctive and well made but production figures would be small.

RIGHT: Dormobile were still a major force in campervans but had its two popular GRP coachbuilts, this one – the Land Cruiser – and the Debonair. The Land Cruiser, based on the new Bedford CF 2.3 litre petrol engine, slept four. The kitchen came with hob and grill but also a fridge and a 54 litre on-board fresh water tank fed the kitchen via an electrically operated pump. Price in 1972 was £1,994; three years later it had nearly doubled with the 1970s inflation and VAT.

The demountable had limited sales in the UK, but Dandy Caravans, the trailer tent manufacturer, tried the market with this three berth placed on the back of the Russian built Moskvitch pick–up car. Priced at £975 in 1972, it was pure budget. Dandy had also built a Commer based coachbuilt motorhome, but few were built. The Dandy Company went back to its successful trailer tent market.

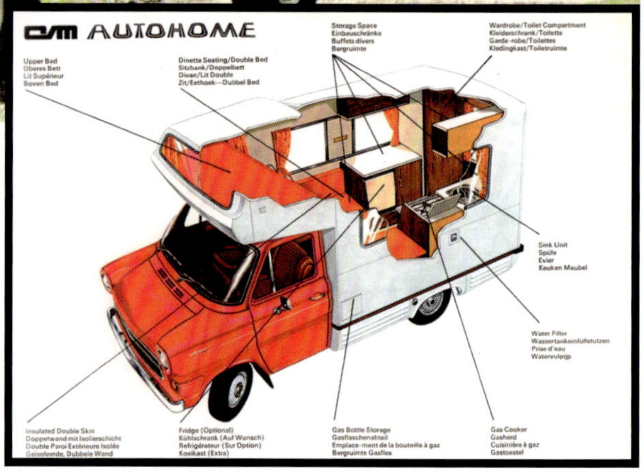

Ci Motorised became Autohomes in 1971, and the new model here was designed by Danish auto engineer Carl Olsen. New modern clean lines inside and out made this an instant success. The caravan section was built separately, then added to the chassis; this meant the coachbuilt section could be exported to fit the German Transit in a Ci factory there. The Ci Autohome was well designed and sold all over Europe. Ford, Bedford and Commer bases were used, offering a selection of engines.

THE 1970s – THE MOTORHOME'S HIGHS AND LOWS 53

ABOVE: Wilsons motorhome dealers were looking at importing more American motorhomes, becoming first to import the Winnebago, but this Dodge based motorhome was classed as the very first 4 x 4 motorhome to be made. Designed for going off into the wilderness, this all terrain motorhome was designed to enable the motorhome user to go most places. Wilsons were looking at getting it priced up for the UK market, but little demand would see it failing with UK buyers.

RIGHT: The Jennings Road Ranger was re-vamped for 1973/4, being based on a Ford Transit Custom 130 or Bedford CF deluxe chassis. It was a luxury motorhome with a spec that included shower, fridge, oven, hot water, and flush loo. Prices began at £3,049 and more options could be added including mains and air conditioning. By 1975, Jennings were no more as the slump in sales hit with the oil crisis and high inflation.

Dormobile launched its new coachbuilt Deauville in 1978 on a Bedford CF using bonded side construction, though the profile looked awkward, being plain especially after the Land Cruiser and Debonair of a few years before. The Deauville was never going to cut it in an ever-growing competitive market place. Within a couple of years, Dormobile would do their best to give the Deauville a revamp to increase sales.

(Top photo) Multicruiser built demountable motorhomes and specials in the mid-1970s; they also did a coachbuilt body on cars such as this Mk3 Cortina 2 litre. This idea was also carried out by Bridport Conversions (bottom half of photo) with the Prince also using various cars such as this Volvo and adding the Austin Maxi to build on a coachbuilt motorhome to the bodywork. (Photos Andrew Jenkinson)

THE 1970s – THE MOTORHOME'S HIGHS AND LOWS

RIGHT: Cotswold had enjoyed a slice of the luxury motorhome market, building quality coachwork and quality interiors. The Caravelle was available in two and four berths, both having rear end lounges, but neither having a washroom, though a Porta loo was supplied in a seat locker. The options list though was quite large with full oven, heater, fridge and extra battery being extras. Cotswold would also become a victim of a changing market and slow down stopping by 1977.

BELOW: An idea of sticking a touring caravan body on a chassis cab was not uncommon in the 1970s. Carlight added this Casalette two berth model on the rear of a Mercedes and offered this as a Carlight motorhome. The idea was that this was also a customer who wanted his Carlight tourer but without having to tow it and have a motorhome. Carlight would later make a complete coachbuilt motorhome but not until the 1990s and then only to special order.

Although Hull was a major caravan producer, there were also several concerns set up making coachbuilt motorhomes utilising the skills of the caravan industry in the area. Pioneer was one such maker; based on Somerset St in Hull they began in 1979 using the Bedford 250 though Fiat and Mercedes were used for the larger models. Full spec included shower, heater, mains electrics, double glazed and on board fresh and waste water tanks. Pioneer only produced for a few years.

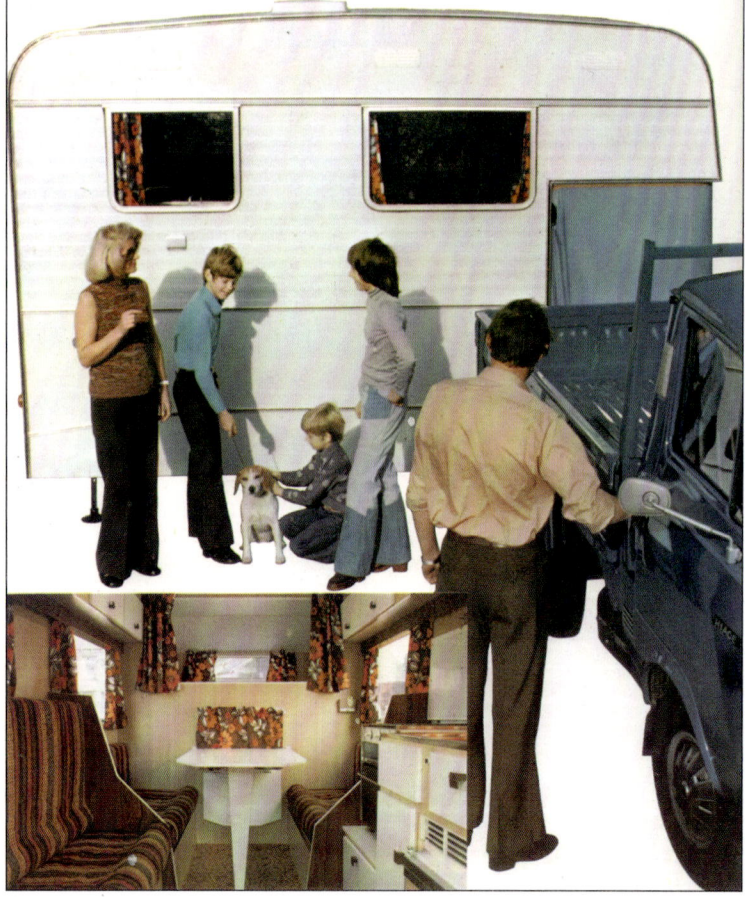

Made in Bradford, Multicruiser began making mainly demountables in 1976 though they would produce one off specials. They took the then new Toyota Hi Ace chassis cab to enter the demountable motorhome market. Multicruiser also used Dodge and Leyland Sherpa as bases. The interiors were quite practical and but also had a slight budget feel, though specification included a gas operated fridge. Mulitcruisers finished by the early 1980s with the recession as many did.

There were convertors who would also put a touring caravan on a chassis such as this Bedford CF from 1974 with a Viking caravan of the same year. Special builds like this were not common but some firms would do this and add the customer's caravan, blending it into to the base vehicle as best they could to make it look aesthetically pleasing. Selling such a conversion on again could be problematic. *(Photo courtesy Andrew Jenkinson)*

In 1976, Colin Reed Motors produced this Custom Camper; this cost around £1,771 in 1976 and was a demountable, one of several builders of this type of motorhome. It slept up to four and buyers had a choice of several interior decors. The base vehicle was the British Leyland Morris Marina pick up model, which was a 508 kgs design.. The construction included a tubular steel framework for the body of the motorhome.

Imported motorhomes were virtually non-existent in the start of the 1970s, especially any from the US. However, Wilsons Motorhomes began importing the Winnebago motorhome into the UK. Wilsons brought in the smaller models, but these were well equipped with fridge, heater, full shower/flush loo, washroom and hot and cold water pumped through. Although Wilson's bought in the more basic models, they still had a high specification; cost was around £4,675 in 1971.

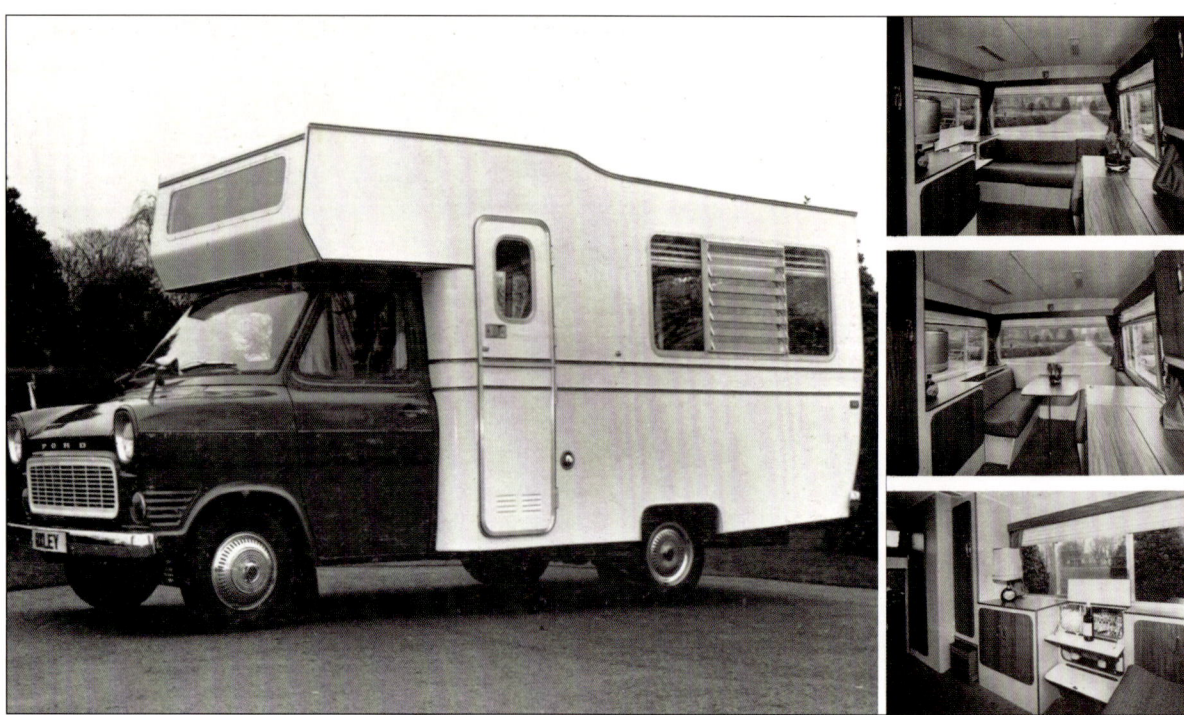

Small concerns were much in evidence in motorhome manufacture; in the early 1970s, Oxley Coachcraft produced these rather nicely finished off motorhomes mainly on the Ford Transit. The louvered windows date it, though this is the Kingston 1974/5 model year. It interestingly offered a rear end L-shaped lounge area and was based on a Ford Transit and slept four. Oxley were one of many new motorhome concerns in the Hull area.

Newlander Motorhomes were another Hull maker that became a user of the then new Toyota Hi Ace chassis using a 1.6 litre petrol engine; this produced 68bhp. Newlander began in 1975 and became a popular range and included fridge, oven and shower as part of the spec. Main exterior image is the two-berth end kitchen. Interior insert is the four-berth version – layout is based on a touring caravan four-berth 3.80m in length but with no toilet compartment.

Hilton were another 1970s newcomer in the growing coachbuilt motorhome market; they were a luxury coachbuilder being made in Douglas, Isle of Man, using mainly VW's LT base, plus Ford, Fiat, Bedford and Leyland but also they used the Toyota Hi Ace with shower, mains electrics, fridge, heater, flush loo, eye-level oven and crafted hand built furniture. The Hiltons were exported to Belgium, and Germany as well as mainland Britain.

There was a growing amount of motorhome dealerships in this decade. Turners, Wilsons, Marquis, Perry's Godfrey Davis, Greens and here Madison's. The company sold cars originally in Southport, selling campervans and motorhomes from 1970. By 1973/4 they had bought new premises at Clifton near Preston where a showroom was built and a large forecourt complete with a petrol station too. Madison's grew and organised customer weekend motorhome rallies with entertainment provided!

Photo of part of the Madison's forecourt in the late 1970s. The site became an importer for Hymer Motorhomes and Tabberts in the next decade, in modern times it still sells motorhomes and touring caravans with owners Preston Caravans and Motorhomes and the site has been extended but the original accessory shop and showroom still exist. *(Photo courtesy John Lunt)*

THE 1970s – THE MOTORHOME'S HIGHS AND LOWS

Wilsons were the biggest dealers in the UK and Europe and had an export market for individual customers. This image shows a Bluebird Highwayman being loaded to be sent to its awaiting buyer in Europe; they sold new but also used motorhomes too and exported as far as New Zealand. Wilsons would move to just car sales and is now a major car dealership.

1979 and the biggest motorhome manufacturer Ci Group were constantly developing their proven models such as this Bedford based MK3 version. The company had two factories at Poole with four production lines making them the biggest motorhome producer in Europe. They exported from the Poole factory as well as sending Autohomes bodies out in kit form to Germany for assembly. Ci went into liquidation in December 1982, with recession hitting them hard. A management buyout saw Autohomes UK emerge, still based at the same production plant.

Autosleeper had been a convertor from the early 1960s near Broadway. They became successful for producing quality interiors and practical design. Autosleeper went into the coachbuilt market in 1976 with this Bedford based motorhome. Using a mixture of GRP mouldings and coach building, this family layout had a rear entrance door. This model would be the springboard for the 1980s Autosleeper coachbuilts that proved popular in the luxury motorhome market.

European motorhomes were a Hull maker from the ashes of the 1960s Paralian motorhome re-named Tourstar. By 1974 they were part of European Caravans A-Line Caravans division a company that had expanded fast in the 1970s. A-Line took European and also designed and built a new range of motorhomes named Adventura. The European Sundowner was launched for 1974 using the Bedford with a 2.2 petrol engine. The styling was distinctive with GRP moulded roof and combined aluminium side panels.

Dormobile though mainly a campervan maker had seen success in the motorhome market with its Debonair and Bedouin models. The New World (designed by Ogle–Tom Karens Company) was based on the Toyota Hi Ace and was seen in 1973 as a modern design blending GRP with the cab and large overhead cab window. It wasn't well received, having handling problems and sales were slow. Dormobile were now part of smokeless fuel company Coalite and there had been changes within the company.

A-Line Caravans Adventura motorhomes were launched for 1975 on Bedford CF chassis and soon became well established, with the range being added to on this success. By 1977, this Bedford based model could sleep up to six, while the Ford Transit and other Bedford based model slept four. Three models were produced for that model year – classed as mid-priced motorhomes, they had hot water and gas operated fridge and used 12 volt strip lights for night illumination.

Another demountable maker in 1974 – the Coche Cama demountable motorhome was made near Southport. Using a GRP body shell, the makers were keen to tell potential customers this was a durable unit that was designed to be placed on a Bedford 1,270kg chassis cab. It came with four jacks to support and leave the caravan body on site. This small maker didn't last long, though considering this market was niche there were several UK makers still involved.

Hull was becoming a fast-expanding area for coachbuilt motorhomes (due to skills developed in the caravan industry) and another such make was Hi Line in 1977 by Humberside Interiors based at Grovehill Beverley an area well known for static, tourer and now motorhome manufacturing. The Hi Line was a luxury motorhome and came with a full specification, including a rare fitted Alde wet heating system. It used a Mercedes 306 chassis cab which powered by a none turbo diesel engine while the Hi Line came with mains electrics as standard.

THE 1970s – THE MOTORHOME'S HIGHS AND LOWS

Romahome concentrated on small motorhomes and using GRP moulded bodies. Island Plastics, based in the Isle of Wight, produced this in the late 1970s on a Honda 350cc petrol engine. It was demountable and was designed by Barry Stimson who would be responsible for more of Island Plastics micro coachbuilt motorhomes. Not aimed at the mass market, reviews of the time said the Honda bobbed along nicely and the Romahome was roomy for its size!

An idea that wasn't new but one the Apex Plant Co decided to use in 1973. Using a Ford Transit Custom, a caravan (a Lynton Scimitar in this case) was attached and specification added to the caravan such as fridge, all 12 volt lighting, hot water, shower and fresh water tank were part of the spec and buyers could opt for a diesel engine over a petrol and interestingly an LPG conversion – the Apex cost £3,000

Cotswold in the early 1970s launched super luxury models such as the Concord 2, using a Mercedes 408 2.2 litre petrol engine or optional diesel. This luxury coachbuilt motorhome built by Ken Stephens Caravans near Cheltenham was a super-sized motorhome for two designed to travel long distances for weeks at a time. It had superb quality woodwork and a large practical kitchen with ample storage. Cotswold would stop production by 1976. Ken Stephens concentrated on selling touring caravans.

OPPOSITE ABOVE: In mid-1976, Ci motorised revamped the long selling Highwayman using new bonded side walls and offering a new more modern interior. Ci would update and improve on a regular basis keeping abreast of the competition. On the new Highwayman Ci now offered it on the recent Leyland Sherpa chassis cab. The Sherpa was in fact to become a popular choice by many makers as a base vehicle.

OPPOSITE BELOW: Richard Holdsworth had begun around 1967 converting campervans. The company grew as the Holdsworth name became known for good design and also good workmanship with solid build quality. With the popularity of the coachbuilt motorhome, Holdsworth decided by 1978 to look at this sector which they felt was an area to next move into. They used the Leyland Sherpa as a base unit and designed an overhead cab bed family motorhome establishing them in this sector.

THE 1970s – THE MOTORHOME'S HIGHS AND LOWS

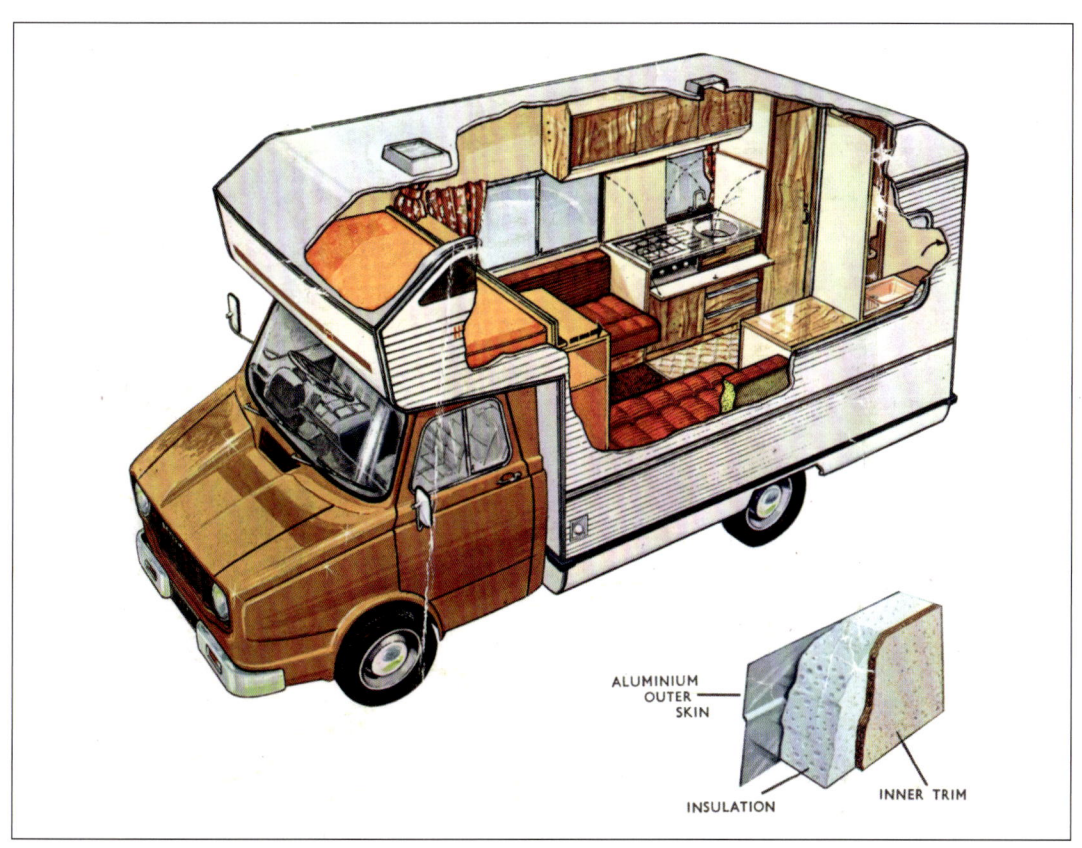

68 A VISUAL HISTORY OF MOTORHOMES: PHOTOGRAPHS FROM THE 20s TO MODERN DAY

ABOVE: Ci was always the best at self-publicity in caravans, campervans and motorhomes they produced. The motorised division for a while had track days where they demonstrated the motorhomes and campervans for the following season. This image was taken in 1974 and general Press organisations were invited to look and drive a vehicle around the test track and report their findings in magazines and national press. Ci was always keen to try new avenues of publicity which they often did successfully.

OPPOSITE ABOVE: In 1977/8, Scotland's largest caravan dealership, Perthshire Caravans, also went into the motorhome market by producing their own coachbuilt models. The new motorhomes were named Auto Cruiser and used Ford's Transit as shown, along with Bedford and Dodge chassis cabs. Priced at £7,000, the simple profile coachbuilt looking motorhome had hot water, fridge, split charging unit, extractor hood and other spec. The Auto cruiser slept four with a rear dinette and central kitchen with wardrobe/washroom opposite.

OPPOSITE BELOW: Avalon based at Cottingham near Hull were caravan manufacturers established in the early 1970s. By 1977/8 they were branching into motorhomes with this Concorde model, based on a Ford Transit. Motorhomes were now including fridges, electrically operated water pumps, hot water as customers demanded. The Avalon Concorde had typically 1970s interior decor using teak photo veneer and pine wood decor. It all sounds grim now, but it was fashionable back then.

THE 1970s – THE MOTORHOME'S HIGHS AND LOWS   69

Ci Motorised factory at Poole around 1974/5 making the caravan body sections for the Ci Autohomes, which were designed to then be attached to any of the popular chassis of the time. Many were exported to Ci's German plant making the Poole factory the biggest producer of motorhomes and campervans in this era. The next decade would see dramatic changes in the company's circumstances, the halcyon days would be over as recession hit, sadly splitting the Ci group up, no longer the giant it once was.

Dandy Caravans, the successful camping trailer makers in Wigan, also went into motorhome manufacture in 1973/4. Based on a Commer unit, it slept four. The unusual feature was its structure using steel 2cm framework making the side walls slimmer than normal coachbuilts. This allowed that little extra space inside. The design looked quite boxy, and the company would eventually concentrate on its trailer tents not getting involved in motorhomes again.

4
1980 TO 2000 ADVANCES IN MOTORHOME DESIGN AND POPULARITY

The 1970s had proved a volatile period in the motorhome's history, with the oil crisis and the rise of inflation plus the introduction of Value Added Tax on caravans and motorhomes in 1973. For a while, sales were hit but by the mid to late 1970s, though names such as Jennings, Hilton and Cotswold had stopped production, new names were appearing and Hull was becoming a hotspot as some caravan manufacturers such as A-Line went into motorhome production and small companies would crop up, several around Beverley. The new decade would see a major slump and Caravans International, the giant of the industry in Europe, would see sales drop and cost double.

The caravan side of the business which included Sprite, Eccles, Europa and Fairholme suffered with the Bluebird holiday homes division being sold off in 1980 back to its original founder/ owner Bill Knott maker of BK holiday homes. In the tail end of 1982 with Caravans International crashing (The touring caravan side was rescued) the motorised division Ci Autohomes shut in 1982 with a very uncertain future. By 1992 Autohomes UK was bought out by Elddis Caravans and Motorhomes who after a few years dropped the Autohome name.

This new decade of the 1980s witnessed several caravan manufacturers turn to motorhomes; Elddis in 1985, Swift 1985/6 and Compass Caravans 1982/3 and small Lancashire maker Lunar Caravans in 1983/4 . The mini boom from 1984 to the early 1990s saw new designs with more aerodynamics used as GRP moulded panels became more common in design and construction of the motorhome. There were new bases such as the Talbot Express and Fiats Ducato and this period would see the rise of the diesel engine being used, especially as this period saw a big development in turbo diesel engines, making them more powerful and yet economical too. All these developments would see the further progress in the design of the motorhome and its new status grow with new sales climbing each year.

This period also saw the rise of imported makes too, such as Tabbert, Hymer, Eriba, Rapido, Adria, Dethleffs, and Pilote and more over the coming years. Dealers such as Turners and Wilsons went out of motorhomes. There was growth in the dealership networks as older established smaller motorhome dealers grew, such as Bromley Motorhome Centre in Kent and Marquis that would begin an expansion plan. Other dealers that emerged in this era were Todd's at Preston selling trailer tents as they moved into motorhomes.

The 1990s also would see more changes, with larger designs using a tag axle while new bases from Renault, VW and Peugeot and Mercedes offered the motorhome buyer more comfortable driving experiences. With the shows that were seeing increasing motorhome makes appearing the popularity of motorhomes had increased to the 1970s levels. Caravan producers Swift now had a dedicated motorhome plant and design division, Swift having success with its Kon-Tiki range in Sweden. Elddis also had big success with its range of Autoquest's motorhomes and Compass Caravans with their Drifter and Calypso.

By the end of the 1990s, the dealer special motorhome would be seen as manufacturers adopted a range of motorhomes with extra kit for certain dealers. The motorhome was back on top as a main leisure vehicle especially in Europe and of course in America. Caravanners who didn't want to tow any more still wanted to do the hobby so a motorhome for many was an ideal choice, especially for continental touring. Air conditioning was an option that higher up models had, along with microwaves and TV aerials and blown air heating by gas and electricity.

Layouts also changed dramatically, with the side door being the most popular entrance while the fixed bed and bunks would also become popular into the late 1990s. New suspension systems and chassis extensions by Al-Ko would be used. The motorhome offered more appeal than ever but, as mentioned, the Ci badge disappeared except for an Italian import that had been part of the old original Ci group the Italian arm set up and soon carved a market out for themselves in the UK. So this would also see the demise of Dormobile, once the biggest maker in the 1960s; its factory shut and was basically flattened to be redeveloped though a specialist company called Dormobile restores and has parts for Dormobiles. The company has recently begun manufacturing campervans, resurrecting the Dormobile brand.

Dormobile was in 1980 going through a tricky period and they had lost a lot of their market share. They were still holding onto the Deauville in 1981, this one pictured using the Sherpa chassis. The profile hadn't improved much, and the layout still stayed the same with rear door entry and the profile hadn't much improved since its launch in the late 1970s. The Deauville cost from £9,340 to £10,000, depending which chassis they used, though Ford and Bedfords were available. It was to be the last coachbuilt motorhome Dormobile launched before the company folded and the once large Kiln Lane factory closed.

Adria, the former Yugoslavian caravan manufacturer, had begun in 1965 and by 1970 were exporting caravans into most of Europe, including the UK. By the early 1980s, their caravan sales were at an all-time high. It was in the mid-1980s that they launched their Adria Adraitik, using a Talbot chassis. The new motorhome had resemblances to the Adria touring caravans in exterior finish and the Adria Blue, also the new Adria motorhome had a good specification to attract UK buyers. The new Adria also came with a space saving fold up loo!

When Ci Autohomes went out of business in 1982, a new company, Autohomes UK was born. The company launched the micro coachbuilt on the Bedford Rascal micro pick-up. Unlike Romahome's, this was not a demountable. Sleeping two, this micro coachbuilt caught the buying public's attention and it was selling well with an owners' club being formed. By 1988 15-20 Bambis were being built weekly, with demand high. Elddis also launched its new micro motorhome, virtually identical to the Bambi, naming it Nipper in 1990.

Lancashire motorhome dealership Madison's, also did their own branded motorhomes such as this model, the Freedom. The Freedom was aimed at the entry level market but was also a detachable design. This idea was not very popular in the UK but several other manufacturers produced them. The Freedom's base vehicle was a communist bloc built FSO. These were cars that looked like the Ladas of their time while the FSO was in fact an old Fiat 124 design. The Freedom was designed to be cheap to buy at £4,995 in the early mid 1980s. *(Photo courtesy of John Lunt)*

The Elddis Nipper was launched for the 1990s, virtually copying the Autohomes UK Bambi concept. The Bambi had proved very popular, and the Nipper was to replicate this, however the Nipper wasn't as popular; although the Elddis was almost the same design, it seemed the Bambi had created a loyal following. The Nipper's interior felt spacious for its size but also it had a bed above the cab just as the Bambi. The Elddis ironically took over the Bambi when they bought out Autohomes UK in 1992.

In 1980, the A-Line Adventura was sold using the Ford Transit chassis as well as Bedford and Leyland. This motorhome range was still selling well, even though this period of time saw a massive drop in sales generally. The Adventura production would be moved to Carlton Caravans – confusingly they were marketed under A-Line, European Caravans division and Carlton Caravans – the 4/6 berth model cost £10,265 and came equipped with fridge, heater double glazing and shower and hot water. Production stopped in 1984.

Avalon Caravans, makers of the Concord from 1977/8, had by 1981 increased their motorhome range to four models, all using several base vehicles such as the Toyota Hi Ace, Ford Transit, Bedford CF and Mercedes 200. The Mercedes would become more popular amongst motorhome manufacturers as a base. Avalon had moved to a new factory in Hull, but the recession of this period saw the company fail, like so many others.

Ci Autohomes were still in the main top sellers in 1980/1, introducing new models such as the fully revised Ci Bedouin, a new look for the 1980s but some quality problems ensured and with sales generally depressed production had been cut back with the parent company cutting back. The heady days of Autohomes' large production figures with exports was dwindling. With heavy borrowings, even models such as this modern looking Bedouin could not help revive the giant Ci group.

Lunar Caravans came into motorhomes in 1984 with its Roadsters sold through Don Amott Leisure in Derbyshire. This was the first introduction of Lunar into motorhome manufacturing. The Lunars were based on the Mercedes 270D and produced in three layouts by 1985. The specification included full mains electrics, shower, heating, spotlights and several power sockets and extractor fan. The Roadsters were renamed Roadstars later on and marked a successful introduction into motorhomes for Lunar as a brand.

GT Motorised was a Hull based company in the early 1980s who were looking at taking on the American motorhomes that were beginning to come into the UK in greater numbers. Their idea was to build large motorhomes in a style based on the American models. However, GT were selling their motorhomes at several thousand pounds cheaper and yet still offering all the luxury accustomed with the US models. Based on Fiat's OM75 lorry chassis, the Florida model here cost £12,000.

Autohomes UK was operating in a smaller factory, but they were developing new models such as the Excalibur and Merlin. Based on the recently launched Talbot Express 1300 with 2 litre petrol engine a diesel was optional. Autohomes had won several awards in 1984 with their new motorhomes commencing production in late 1983. The two models available with two different layouts by 1984 became the top selling motorhomes in the UK – pictured is the Excalibur MK2 and Merlin which brought back some of the former glory days of the original Ci days.

In the mid-1980s, Bessacarr Caravans also saw the rise in motorhome sales and designed a coachbuilt using the new Talbot Express. This was named the Bessacarr Auto Cruise, a fully equipped coachbuilt that had an end kitchen and centre lounge with a bed in the overhead cab. Bessacarr was based at Rawmarsh and the company concentrated on their twin axle luxury caravans which were selling well. The Auto Cruise name became a new motorhome manufacturer based in Mexborough from 1988.

The Ci Highwayman from 1981 had been refreshed using the latest Sherpa but it was all too late for the old Ci Autohomes. Costing £8,824 in 1981, the new Highwayman was still seen as good value, with many customers being owners of older Highwayman models trading up to the latest version. The specification was good and sides were bonded and windows were double glazed.

1980 TO 2000 ADVANCES IN MOTORHOME DESIGN AND POPULARITY

ABOVE: In 1983, Swift Caravans were busy designing a motorhome, a first step into this market. Using a Mercedes, the first motorhome was built based on the firm's Swift Cottingham touring caravan model of that year. This gave the designers at Swift a basis on which to begin serious development of a new range of motorhomes for the UK market. Through 1984, the company began designing a motorhome that was to use GRP aerodynamic mouldings from Swift's own glass fibre manufacturing plant. *(Photo courtesy of Swift Group)*

RIGHT: By 1985, Swift had designed their smart looking new motorhome, Kon-Tiki – a model that was named the 600. The interior was very luxurious and based on their Swift luxury Corniche caravan, rear end had L-shaped seating and side washroom; it also used the latest Talbot Chassis. The new Swift motorhome was well received and within a couple of years the Kon Tiki was selling well at home and abroad. *(Photo courtesy of Swift Group)*

Daytona motorhomes were a small maker near Rotherham South Yorkshire. The company built coachbuilt motorhomes using the popular Ford Transit and Bedford chassis cabs. Bonded construction for the sides was used while Bofors Swedish double-glazed windows were used. The company would also just supply the shell with entrance door for £4,950. The company had been around for ten years doing special conversions and custom builds.

Hymermobile S Class – the German manufacturer that was to dominate Europe by buying other brands. These luxury all-season motorhomes were quality built units that were hitting the UK via then large Lancashire dealers Madison's. Hymermobile motorhomes were well equipped and soon a loyal following was established, and Madison's were importing them direct from Germany and soon buyers would travel to view and pick up directly from the importers.

1980 TO 2000 ADVANCES IN MOTORHOME DESIGN AND POPULARITY

Auto Sleeper had introduced their first motorhome in 1976/7 and from this in 1982 they set about a new design using GRP moulded panels for the early 1980s. Auto Sleeper brought in designer William Towers, a leading stylist who had worked for Aston Martin. The new Bedford based coachbuilt had an end kitchen and corner shower room and a side dinette that made into a double. It could sleep up to four and was named the SV100 and instantly won motorhome Industry awards.

The 1980s was the decade of imported makes into the UK and French maker Pilote were one of many to arrive here in 1988. The R380 pictured slept four and came with a very high specification including flyscreens and blinds while it used the Talbot Express 1400 chassis cab using a 2 litre petrol engine. Pilote had begun as a caravan maker but by the late 1970s went on to make motorhomes. Pilote found themselves a niche in the UK.

Hymers all lined up in Preston Docks awaiting to be picked up and taken a few miles down the road to Madison's dealership. In 1980, Hymer merged with Eriba while in 1986 they were the first manufacturer to offer a six year water ingress warranty and in this year, they built their ten thousandth motorhome. Mercedes chassis were used to add to the luxury feel of the Hymermobile motorhomes. The brand offered more layouts as the years went by and is still a top-quality German motorhome. *(Photo courtesy John Lunt)*

Elddis Caravans had been bought out by A.B.I. Caravans in 1973. After the mid-1970s' slump in caravans, Elddis looked at building motorhomes. By the mid-1980s they produced their first motorhomes and after a few years they produced a three layout range with an A Class motorhome design named the Auto King. This new motorhome for 1989 was the head of the Elddis three range line up. By the end of the 1980s, Elddis, like Swift, were firmly established as a motorhome manufacturer.

Glendale had started in 1976 and ran for some years before the company finished. The previous owner began another company at Hull named Eagle, but the Glendale name was to be bought by Irish maker C&V who had made van conversions but went onto coachbuilt motorhomes sending components over to Hull to assemble into the new Glendale motorhomes. This Ford Transit based family four-berth named the Golf (pictured) offered a well specified motorhome on a Ford Transit base.

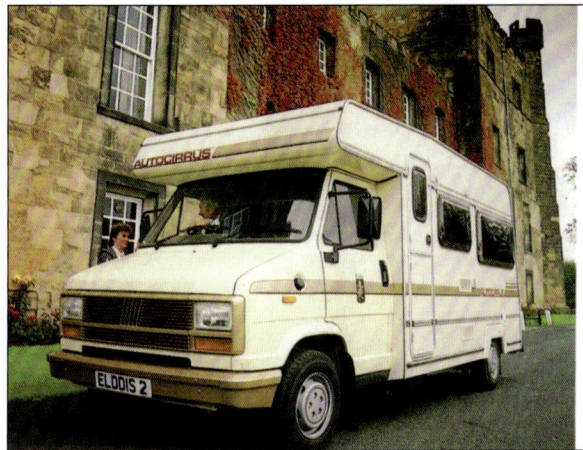

Based on the latest Talbot Express, the Elddis Autocirrus was the base range of Elddis. However, for 1988 a four-berth was added to the two-berth layout. The specification included mains electrics, fridge and heater plus a shower and also plenty of storage, even in the family model. The exterior included colour co-ordinated bumpers and for that period looked modern and stylish.

Auto-Trail motorhomes began back in Grimsby in 1984 by ex-Abbey caravans /Mustang Caravans Bill Boasman. The company began with just a few repairs, then manufactured coachbuilt motorhomes and by the end of the 1980s Auto Trail soon found themselves in demand. The Chieftain in the picture was on a Mercedes 307D and had an L-shaped rear kitchen and side settee pull out double bed plus two free-standing armchairs and roof mounted Electrolux air con unit.

Multicruiser by 1984 had moved to a new factory in Hull and here produced their compact demountable coachbuilt motorhome for a pick such as a Toyota/Datsun. The unit came with full double-glazed windows and was also fully insulated. Entry was by a rear glazed door, while four could also sleep and sit in the dining area. No washroom was fitted, just bare essentials such as cooker and grill and sink with cold only water supply. Prices varied on base vehicle but averaged around £3,000 in 1983.

1980 TO 2000 ADVANCES IN MOTORHOME DESIGN AND POPULARITY

RIGHT: CRV was another Hull based motorhome manufacturer producing in 1984 eleven coachbuilts. Using the main bases from Ford, Fiat and Bedford they also used the Mitsubishi L300 van base for their Suntourer – (one pictured is an export model) which cost £10,177 and slept four. Aimed more at the entry level range it still came fitted with a fridge but only a twin burner hob. Interior styling was simple, but it did come equipped with mains electrics, heater and fresh and waste water tanks.

BELOW: Hymers Importers Madison's were bringing a smaller range of Hymers to catch another area of the motorhome market in 1987. These more compact models meant that they were more affordable with a price tag of £13,978 this Hymercamp 47 was based on a diesel Mitsubishi L300 in left hand drive only. Hymer used a galvanised steel profile frame then bonded sides and roof. The Hymers were imported into the UK with a German specification which was high in equipment and build quality.

Auto-Sleeper would improve and refresh its coachbuilt range such as the Talisman II in 1987; this couple's motorhome came with end kitchen and offside corner shower room and central dinette. Very high equipment levels included full heating, mains, fridge, swivel front cab seats and the Talisman II even came with crockery supplied. The Auto-Sleeper glass fibre monocoque ranges became classics and also were sought after on the used market keeping prices firm.

Apollo Motorhomes in Rochdale were one of these small convertors with a niche following. They also made standard coachbuilt motorhomes and specialised in detachable models such as this 1998 410D model which slept up to four, designed to go on the backs of pick ups such as Isuzu (as image) Tata, Nissan, Vauxhall and Toyota. The Apollo came with shower, heater, fridge and mains electrics. Apollo made several different demountables over the years, as well as conventional models using the Fiat Ducato.

1980 TO 2000 ADVANCES IN MOTORHOME DESIGN AND POPULARITY

Compass Caravans ex-Elddis founders Ray and Siddle Cook had been making Compass caravans from 1979 and by 1982/3 they produced their Drifter and Clipper models. By the 1990s, Compass were firmly established as another Caravan manufacturer turned motorhome maker. Names such as Drifter (pictured) Calypso, Commodore, Clipper became familiar in motorhome circles. Interiors were traditional and in 1994 five Drifter models were listed, Compass would buy out Herald Motorhomes with Compass selling to Explore Group–Elddis.

Herald Motorhomes were short lived, sadly, but that wasn't down to their poor design or quality, all based on the latest Ford Transit with the 2.5 diesel engine with a chassis designed by Ford for motorhome manufacturers. Herald was the new motorhome manufacturer to emerge from the Ci Autohomes/Autohomes UK original factory premises. Autohomes UK were sold to Elddis in 1992 and the factory shut at 59 Old Wareham Road Poole. Using staff from these two companies, Herald ironically shut down after Compass purchased the company a few years later.

Super luxury caravan builder Carlight Caravans had built all types of specials over the years. Based at Sleaford in the early 1990s, they produced this coachbuilt Carlight motorhome using a Mercedes 208D. This motorhome was handbuilt by a small team with craftsmanship built real veneer wood furniture. Built as a couples motorhome, it could sleep four in the overhead cab. It came with such items as Wedgewood bone china and lead crystal glasses! Cost in 1990/1 was £33,350 – few were built!

Swift had progressed dramatically over the years and by 1998 they had an A Class motorhome in production with two models. Priced at £50,195 they were luxury motorhomes. Based on Fiat Ducato with Al-Ko chassis, the Bel-Airs were a major step in Swift's motorhome line up. But the two models had limited success and were dropped, with not many being produced. It was an area that Swift didn't venture into again and concentrated on its highly successful Kon-Tiki range Sundance and Royale coachbuilts.
(Photo courtesy Swift Group)

Island Plastics, who had made demountables with a GRP body, had by the early 1990s got designer Barry Stimson to design a new micro coachbuilt using a Citroen C15 diesel 1.8 and used it for the basis of its new motorhome. Winning awards for its design, the new Citroen Romahome carved itself a niche in the smaller motorhome market. This boasted headroom of 1.9m, while the furniture was made from moulded GRP. A low top version followed (named Hi Top) that could be extended on site.

The American imports were gaining popularity mainly among those who wanted the ultimate in motorhome ownership. These usually had a slide out section on the side. The Swinger here from top American manufacturer Georgie Boy was imported with other brands by Midland International American Motorhomes in Coventry. Available on either a Ford or Chevy chassis the 1995 Swinger was available in seven layouts. Super specification meant owners were left not wanting anything!

Marquis Motorhomes established in 1973 had by the early 1990s begun to expand, opening new branches such as the Berkshire branch being opened by the local Mayor in 1991/2. Marquis merged with Auto Sleeper and also took on several more franchises over the years, including reintroducing Spanish Benimar motorhomes in the UK back in 2015. Marquis/Auto sleeper also became part of the giant leisure Group Trigano, who also bought out Adria caravans and motorhomes.

By 1990, Richard Holdsworth had seen the Ranger evolve into a smart looking modern motorhome. Motorhomes since the mid-1980s had become far sportier looking, especially with the newer bases. Holdsworth became users of the Renault Traffic, which was a petrol unit but as the 1990s progressed, motorhome makers moved to diesel, ousting petrol altogether. The Ranger was just as modern inside as it was out, with Ikea-styled interior lockers and kitchen units.

1980 TO 2000 ADVANCES IN MOTORHOME DESIGN AND POPULARITY

Elddis had, like Swift, become a dedicated motorhome manufacturer and by 1990 were producing some attractive motorhomes that were proving more popular into this decade. The Autocirrus was available in three layouts and were built onto the latest Mercedes 208D. Interestingly, the Mercedes and VW bases in this era were popular choices for many motorhome manufacturers. The Elddis used many GRP exterior panels to provide better streamlining and smarter profiles.

Lunar had by the end of the 1990s established themselves as not just caravan manufacturers but also firmly in the motorhome market too. The Roadstar 570L pictured here was based on a Fiat 2.8 Tdi and features a rear L shaped lounge area. The interiors were based on the company's luxury Delta caravan range offering rich wood finish lots of storage plus a high specification. The 570L would sleep four but mainly couples bought the 570 because they could also take the grandchildren away or use the overhead bed for storage.

Compass were well established by 1998 for producing quality motorhomes and also launching new models such as the new Caravel based on the then new Mercedes Sprinter chassis. Compass launched its luxury motorhome which was fully equipped and which was fashionable in the 1990s, lots of wood finish and twin overhead roof lockers; a main locker, then a smaller one built in underneath. Belgian sprung upholstery adding to the luxury ambience. The Caravel was also available on the VW LT35 which sliced £3,000 off the Mercedes based version.

Auto Sleepers Ravenna was based on a Peugeot and this two-berth side kitchen motorhome in 1999 looked sleek and was typically designed the way the Auto Sleepers coachbuilt range was in this period. The Ravenna also came with an L-shaped rear lounge plus a well-equipped shower room and good storage. The interior decor was in blue with the light oak furniture blending in well. The Auto sleeper coachbuilt range was popular with its classic styling.

1980 TO 2000 ADVANCES IN MOTORHOME DESIGN AND POPULARITY

Micro coachbuilts have always been niche, though the Autohomes Bambi proved the exception in this sector. However, the new smaller diesel vehicles such as the Citroen C15D were ideal for small coachbuilt motorhomes such as this one from Venture motorhomes which was founded by ex-Trophy Caravans staff and the later 90s the company was named Nu Venture Campers. The Venture pictured was named 'Baby'; it was well equipped including heating, cooker and fridge plus the overhead cab could be used as a child's bed.

Swift were also using VW as a base and on the latest new 1998 Royales complete with a new GRP roof front roof section. The new 1998 Royales now used a fully bonded construction and the exterior also had new moulded copings. The last decade had seen the gradual move from aluminium side panels to using GRP sides for a tougher and more resistant finish. In the early days of this, the panels were more prone to fade with age compared with modern GRP wall side's finishes now.

5

2000-24

The last two decades saw some remarkable changes in the motorhome. Some of the old makes that had been around in the 1960s and 1970s had long gone over time. The 1980s would witness a slump in the early part resulting in some major losses in the motorhome industry. American imports would try and take a hold in the UK market but would prove more of a niche market than anything larger in sales. The new Talbot Express, Renault Traffic and Fiat and Peugeot coming out with new van bases meant that the coachbuilder of motorhomes was becoming spoilt for choice.

The other van makes such as Ford and Bedford would be improved further, though Bedford would pull out by the 2000's. Mercedes and VW would also become more of force in the motorhome's chassis / cab market. Hull's caravan industry in the 1960s and 1970s would in the mid-1970s see a rise in small motorhome concerns starting up. Some made an impact such as Pioneer and Newlander while caravan makers such as A – Line Caravans would in 1975 begin motorhome production. In the 1970s such companies as Godfrey Davis Group had gone into selling caravans in the 1970s but also took on motorhome sales later.

There had been new dealership concerns springing up too with some of the older ones such as Turners of London seemingly just fading away Even once-large dealership Wilsons had moved back into car sales and no longer dealt with motorhomes. Gailey had moved into motorhome sales along with its caravan and static caravans but by the early 1980s the Gailey Group had collapsed, closing most of its depots. Marquis though who had begun in 1973, would slowly expand as the 1980s and 1990s progressed and by the Millenium to the present see massive expansion.

Motorhomes were also to see more specification added, especially with the event of mains electrics being introduced on caravan sites by the early 1990's. Better insulation was introduced with bonded sides and sandwich insulated floors. Showers and fridges were commonly fitted and although the demountable motorhome was never popular, it still didn't stop several small makers such as Apollo and CRV entering this market. The 1980s saw the demise of Caravans International for the company to be split up and sold off. Ci Autohomes was rescued and renamed Autohomes UK stopping at the old premises.

The new Autohomes Company did well with its new models Merlin and Talisman not to mention a new micro motorhome named the Bambi. new maker named Herald was formed again using the old original Bluebird/Autohomes works. The company made up from old Autohome UK workers and for several years enjoyed success before being bought out by Compass Caravans and Motorhomes some years later shutting the Poole factory and transferring all Herald production to Compass in Durham

Layouts would change over the years with more designs with end kitchens and by the late 1990s the fixed bed had come into its own becoming popular in the UK by the mid-2000s. The 1980s had seen imported makes coming in from Europe such as Hymer, Pilote and Adria. Some of these would come into the UK in their country's spec including left hand drive. Also, the choice of engines was becoming more popular; with diesel engines becoming more refined and fitted with turbo slowly saw the petrol engine literally being overtaken by diesel.

The 2000s would see more imports and some becoming well established such as Adria and Hymer now it seemed the imported motorhome was making real headway into the UK marketplace. Swift, Elddis and Compass had moved to motorhome production though all still built caravans. Smaller makers such as Auto Trail had been bought out and sold to ABI Caravans which moved again after ABI went bust in 1998. Trigano a growing European group bought several caravan and motorhome manufacturers and would also buy out the Marquis Group who had some years earlier bought Auto Sleeper motorhomes.

The motorhome market was growing and in the pandemic saw supply problems and a scarcity in motorhome stock. There were more new makes coming in from Europe while established imports expanded their ranges and taking a firm grip on the UK market. Over the years, caravan shows have witnessed more motorhomes and also the dealer special which consists of a maker's base model having added spec and upgraded soft furnishings. The dealer specials began mainly in the mid-1990s and have become a popular choice in modern times for buyers wanting extra specification but at a keener cost.

The diesel has become the most popular engine, but the ongoing EV idea has been experimented with on the motorhome but as yet it's still some years away. With solar panels and LED lighting, the motorhome has evolved into a leisure vehicle that has grown more in popularity over the years. Even the solid branded Caravan Club would have a massive makeover renaming the club The Caravan and Motorhome Club, though motorhomes had been allowed in the Caravan Club since 1967!

From those early vehicles from the 1920s the coachbuilt motorhome has had many ups and downs, almost disappearing for a time after the Second World War. The new breed of vehicles launched in the 1950s paved the way for a new breed of leisure vehicle user. The motorhome then has developed to a sophisticated home on wheels with prices of all budgets. The modern motorhome is growing in popularity with more people discovering the freedom this type of holiday provides, just as those early motorhome users did all those decades ago.

Mc Louis is an Italian maker one of many coming into the UK. This 2004 Lagan was based on a Fiat Ducato chassis and the brand aimed firmly on value. Durable and well-designed, these motorhomes came into the UK and distributed by Don Amott Leisure. Mc Louis were popular because they offered value for money and were also generally well kitted out and well made.

Weinsberg began as camper van maker but as time went on they launched into motorhomes and also caravans. The company was bought out by Tabbert but their impact onto the UK market was minimal. The 2005 Orbiter 591S pictured was available in five layouts and came with the popular rear end garage for storage, a feature that continental buyers favoured. Weinsberg became part of Knaus/Tabbert Group re-launching in the UK in 2015/16 under new ownership.

Benimar is a Spanish manufacturer, being founded in 1974, then making caravans. In 1978 they built their first motorhome on a Mercedes chassis and within a decade were dedicated motorhome manufacturers. By 2002 they became part of the ever-growing Trigano Group being imported into the UK. Pictured is the 2002 Europe 600ST on Fiat chassis priced at £36,500, interiors were well appointed with quality build and styling. Specification included microwave and remotely controlled rear corner steadies plus Alde heating.

Autocruise in 2000 launched its rear door Vista on Peugeot Boxer 2 litre Turbo diesel chassis and was a compact motorhome for two. It still had a well-equipped specification including oven, fridge shower and cassette loo. This compact motorhome was also made as a dealer special with a tie up with Marquis Motorhomes. The compact motorhome was designed for those wanting a coachbuilt but no larger than a camper van conversion.

98 A VISUAL HISTORY OF MOTORHOMES: PHOTOGRAPHS FROM THE 20s TO MODERN DAY

Hymer was to carve a slice of the UK market by the 2000s, again offering a large range of different types and layouts to the UK customer. Hymer also bought out several companies, including UK Elddis Group. In turn, Thor Industries bought Hymer in 2021. Image shows two of Hymers range in 2003, the C class and B class motorhomes available in various trim levels; the choice was vast. Hymer now have various dealerships around the UK.

German manufacturer Burstner was a furniture maker in the 1920s and the skills over the years were to be used in caravan manufacture then motorhomes. The brand has been in the UK for years with its solid well-planned motorhomes. The Elegance range is a luxury A class line up of motorhomes. The styling showed back in 2004 that they had flair and even two decades later still looks a modern motorhome inside and out.

Avondale were a respected caravan manufacturer that went into motorhome manufacture in 2001 with two luxury compact motorhomes, the Seascape and the Seaspirit, based on a Fiat Ducato. Both were influenced on the Auto Sleepers coachbuilts of the time. The interiors were grabbed from the company's luxury bird range of tourers. Layouts were available as two and three berth designs all three layouts having end kitchens. Production was short lived, the firm reverting to concentrating on its touring caravan ranges.

Pre-Elddis involvement, Buccaneer had launched two coachbuilt motorhomes but few were built. With the takeover, the factory was moved to Elddis from Full Sutton near York in the 2000s and here the new luxury Buccaneer motorhomes were redesigned and built using modern methods and by 2001 the new range was ready. The Commodore was, as all Buccaneers, based on Ford's new chassis. Buccaneer wasn't to last long in the motorhome market.

When the original UK Ci group collapsed in late 1982, the company was split and sold off. The Italian factory (opened in 1976) was shut but a management buyout got the company up and running and the caravan side of the business was stopped and motorhome production began. Ci motorhomes were imported into the UK in the 1990s. The 2005 Mizar GTL living model pictured was a seven-berth on a Fiat 2.8 JTD. The Ci range offered family fixed bunk layouts at the right price; they also became part of Trigano.

Elddis, who took over Compass, had launched their entry level Autoquest range in 2001. They also did the same with Compass introducing the Avantgarde range. Using a simple coachbuilt profile and less ornate interiors, prices were kept down. On launch, the Avantgarde 100 pictured cost just over £22,105 aimed at the first time buyer and both the Elddis and Compass ranges sold well. Both were based on the latest Peugeot Boxer 1.9 Tdi. Both ranges became favourites for dealer-based specials.

ABOVE: Dethleffs was one of the first German makers to use Fiats Ducato chassis in 1983. A long-established company, it had a stop start importation in the UK. The company also is under the Hymer Group. The 2003 Advantage was available in a low profile, but the range was a mid-priced line up offering practical design and quality build with a good specification. The Esprit and Globetrotter were other popular Dethleffs ranges imported via Lowdhams Leisure

RIGHT: Mobilvetta has in recent time re-entered the UK market but back in 2002 the name was still not known much in this country. They produced several ranges, this pictured being a 2002 Luna model range. Mobilvetta had another range named Euroyacht which were one of the better sellers in the UK. Design was typical Italian with flair and one of several Italian motorhome manufacturers trying to establish themselves in the UK market. Mobilvetta ranges are now sold through Marquis Group another Trigano member.

The new imports in the early part of the 2000s witnessed a market that offered a more modern European look which was being favoured over the traditional interiors on offer by most UK manufacturers. Swift Group, who had in 2001 acquired the Ace Caravan name from ABI UK, used this brand for a new range of European styled motorhomes. Cool, modern continental interiors were readily accepted. The 2008 Ace Roma came with the continental rear end garage with double bed above and was on the Fiat Ducato. *(Photo Andrew Jenkinson Photography)*

Autocruise was bought by Swift Group and models such as the Startrail pictured were class leading coachbuilt motorhomes from the South Yorkshire maker. Side fixed bed and side corner washroom with front lounge was the layout for this family low profile motorhome. Shortly after, the coachbuilts were to be ended and the Autocruise name was to be used on a range of campervans. Out of the Autocruise demise came Bentley Motorhomes ex –Autocruise staff but Bentley shut a few years later. *(Photo Andrew Jenkinson Photography)*

French maker Chausson began motorhomes in 1980, by the 1990s they had got a reputation for value for money, well-built motorhomes. Imported into the UK from the early 2000s, they built up a following with ranges such as the Welcome, Flash and the Allegro pictured here from 2005 a low profile motorhome. They used Ford, Fiat, Renault and Citroen giving their customers a wide choice of bases. For a short while Chausson stopped being imported but by 2013/14 they were back with a dealer network in the UK

The micro motorhome had evolved to what would be classed as a compact. Nu Venture, a small company in Wigan, used Citroen bases with a diesel engine. Gone by 2005/6 was the plainer coachbuilt profiles, instead new moulded overhead cabs and rear back one piece panels were used, making these compact motorhomes by Nu Venture a smartly styled unit. The Nu Surf pictured in 2009 was an end kitchen front lounge design that has proved a popular layout. *(Photo Andrew Jenkinson Photography)*

Swift launched its entry level Escape range in 2009. This range was to offer a four model line up from £30,445 to £33,245 with the interior cabinet work, borrowed from the Sprite caravan range. Basic equipment levels made this an ideal range to be used by hire fleets. The Escape was based on the Fiat 100 multi jet diesel engine which could be upgraded to the 130. Swift also offered packs to add extras at minimal cost to the customer.

Swift had bought out the Bessacarr Caravan name and in 1997 introduced the name on a range of upmarket motorhomes. The E695 FROM 2010 pictured was one of the most popular in the line up with its large rear lounge area and side kitchen and washroom. The Bessacarrs came with distinctive styling and offered the latest Truma blown air heating. The Bessacarr used the Fiat Ducato and the Bessacarr range would prove a favourite amongst motorhome buyers for some year. *(Photo Andrew Jenkinson Photography)*

Swift launched its Compact Rio range for 2015 to provide a motorhome that was not too large to handle, yet still spacious. The construction was Swift's new non-timber system named Smart which used a water repellent material. The Rio also features a lift up rear back panel for some of the range. The Rio 310 pictured is a 2016 model and featured a full width compact rear washroom and central front lounge area. The Rio range numbered four models in 2016. *(Photo Andrew Jenkinson Photography)*

Wingamm is an Italian small business established around 1977. Wingamm motorhomes are made from GRP and the Micros Plus from 2017 was based on a VWT6 diesel. Wingamm showed how sleek a motorhome can be designed using a one-piece GRP shell. Wingamm had an electric operated drop-down bed in one of their early 1982 Oasi 550 &600 motorhomes as well as a GRP body shell. Wingamm were quite ahead of their time. *(Photo Andrew Jenkinson Photography)*

Auto-Trail were to become part of Trigano Group and the factory was re-built and the Auto-Trail motorhome ranges have over the years been further developed. This 2017 Imala 734 shows Auto-Trail's design flair with pleasing looks inside and out. Launched in 2014 the Imala proved a hit with buyers wanting a stunning design at an affordable cost as well as being practical. *(Photo Andrew Jenkinson Photography)*

Bailey Caravans' first venture into motorhomes was in 2011 with the Approach range. Bailey used their own newly developed construction Alu-Tech, removing timber framing except for the floors. Based on a Peugeot Boxer, the first Baileys were low profile models. Within a few years, the motorhome range had been expanded. For 2017, the Autograph Bailey motorhome showed how the Bailey was evolving. The interiors had improved over the early Baileys and the overall design was distinctive. *(Photo Andrew Jenkinson Photography)*

The Swift Bolero range was a luxury model that reflected on interior design the same type locker design as the Swift Elegance tourer range. Specification was high and this 2016 744PR Black Edition low profile roof line model featured a large rear end lounge area. Based on a Fiat Ducato, the Bolero also had a large side washroom and front offside lounge area. Although the 744 would sleep up to four, couples were said to be the main buyers of this layout. *(Photo Andrew Jenkinson Photography)*

Benimar motorhomes would stop being imported to the UK. The market was seen as not being ideal, though this was to change by 2014/5 when Marquis Motorhomes Group decided to bring back to the UK the Benimar in its low profile form. The Mileo with its classy contemporary interior and high specification has re-established the brand in the UK. This 2016 264 had twin single rear beds. *(Photo Andrew Jenkinson photography)*

Auto Sleeper had developed their new look coachbuilts turning out some good-looking motorhomes. The modern motorhome with the new moulded panel designs were typically used on Auto Sleeper coachbuilts. The Corinium pictured here is a 2016 model and used the side fixed bed design with end washroom. A super spacious motorhome the Corinium had a large front lounge area while overall it lived up to the quality build and finish of the Auto Sleeper motorhome ranges. *(Photo Andrew Jenkinson Photography)*

The dealer special was to launch in the early part of the 1990s and enabled a basic range of a manufacturer to be given extra specification and upgraded soft furnishings chosen by the dealership. Several brands had their entry level models chosen to upgrade to certain dealers' ideas of a special from their dealership. One example is this Elddis Avantgarde, used for dealers Richard Baldwin to build a motorhome to their specification. Named Picasso, this neat motorhome was designed to sell just at this dealership. *(Photo Andrew Jenkinson photography)*

Elddis, now under the Hymer Group, was also using new construction with their motorhome range. They introduced Solid in 2013/14, using fewer screws and more adhesives to help cut down water ingress. The 2017 Encore 285 pictured was one of four layouts featuring twin single beds and end washroom and large front lounge. The Encore was the top of the Elddis motorhome range and included Alde heating, a system that was now a standard fit on luxury models. *(Photo Andrew Jenkinson Photography)*

Swifts 2024 motorhome ranges have been further enhanced and the Voyager has proved a success for the Swift brand. Smart construction and all in house manufactured GRP mouldings enhance the quality and styling of the Voyager 475. Based on Ford's chassis, a chassis that modern motorhome manufacturers have turned to, the Voyager offers so much in specification for the money. Over forty years of motorhome manufacture has seen the Swift become a leader in the UK. *(Photo courtesy of Swift Group)*

Pilote, a French brand that began in 1962 making caravans, had by 1984/5 changed to making motorhomes and they invented the low profile idea. Now a major group of companies, the Joa Camp motorhomes offers the brand's quality at a competitive price but also featuring contemporary interior styling. The 60F (pictured) is a compact fixed bed two-berth built on a Citroen 2.2 HDI engined chassis. Typical modern styling for an entry level motorhome. *(Photo Andrew Jenkinson Photography)*

Laka is an Italian manufacturer that has been present over the years in the UK. Established in 1964 making caravans, the firm moved to motorhome manufacture by the 1980s. Typical Italian design the Laka offers several model ranges and the Kosmo is a low-profile design based on Fiats. The imported motorhome is a common sight on UK roads, with large groups such as Trigano and Hymer owning more brands – the history of the motorhome continues to evolve. *(Photo Andrew Jenkinson Photography)*